Evolutionary Economics and Social Complexity Science

Volume 34

The Japan Association for Evolutionary Economics (JAFEE) always has adhered to its original aim of taking an explicit "integrated" approach. This path has been followed steadfastly since the Association's establishment in 1997 and, as well, since the inauguration of our international journal in 2004. We have deployed an agenda encompassing a contemporary array of subjects including but not limited to: foundations of institutional and evolutionary economics, criticism of mainstream views in the social sciences, knowledge and learning in socio-economic life, development and innovation of technologies, transformation of industrial organizations and economic systems, experimental studies in economics, agent-based modeling of socio-economic systems, evolution of the governance structure of firms and other organizations, comparison of dynamically changing institutions of the world, and policy proposals in the transformational process of economic life. In short, our starting point is an "integrative science" of evolutionary and institutional views. Furthermore, we always endeavor to stay abreast of newly established methods such as agent-based modeling, socio/econo-physics, and network analysis as part of our integrative links. More fundamentally, "evolution" in social science is interpreted as an essential key word, i.e., an integrative and /or communicative link to understand and re-domain various preceding dichotomies in the sciences: ontological or epistemological, subjective or objective, homogeneous or heterogeneous, natural or artificial, selfish or altruistic, individualistic or collective, rational or irrational, axiomatic or psychological-based, causal nexus or cyclic networked, optimal or adaptive, micro- or macroscopic, deterministic or stochastic, historical or theoretical, mathematical or computational, experimental or empirical, agent-based or socio/econo-physical, institutional or evolutionary, regional or global, and so on. The conventional meanings adhering to various traditional dichotomies may be more or less obsolete, to be replaced with more current ones vis-à-vis contemporary academic trends. Thus we are strongly encouraged to integrate some of the conventional dichotomies. These attempts are not limited to the field of economic sciences, including management sciences, but also include social science in general. In that way, understanding the social profiles of complex science may then be within our reach. In the meantime, contemporary society appears to be evolving into a newly emerging phase, chiefly characterized by an information and communication technology (ICT) mode of production and a service network system replacing the earlier established factory system with a new one that is suited to actual observations. In the face of these changes we are urgently compelled to explore a set of new properties for a new socio/economic system by implementing new ideas. We thus are keen to look for "integrated principles" common to the above-mentioned dichotomies throughout our serial compilation of publications. We are also encouraged to create a new, broader spectrum for establishing a specific method positively integrated in our own original way.

Makoto Mizuno

Complex Modeling of Consumer Behavior

Agent-Based Marketing Science

Springer

Makoto Mizuno
School of Commerce
Meiji University
Chiyoda-ku, Tokyo, Japan

ISSN 2198-4204 ISSN 2198-4212 (electronic)
Evolutionary Economics and Social Complexity Science

ISBN 978-4-431-54873-7 ISBN 978-4-431-54874-4 (eBook)
https://doi.org/10.1007/978-4-431-54874-4

This Springer imprint is published by the registered company Springer Nature Japan KK
The registered company address is: Shiroyama Trust Tower, 4-3-1 Toranomon, Minato-ku, Tokyo 105-6005, Japan

Preface

This book offers a distinctive perspective on the application of agent-based modeling in the domain of marketing science, while concurrently presenting the author's own research endeavors. It is noteworthy that this book is part of the Evolutionary Economics and Social Complexity Science series, a choice that may perplex some readers. However, given the significant influence of economics (along with other disciplines such as psychology) on the evolution of marketing science, the inclusion of this book in the series is not unexpected. Economics and marketing science are both concerned with the interaction between firms (sellers) and consumers (buyers) in the market. While economics aims to enhance societal welfare, marketing focuses on the success of individual businesses. Consequently, these disciplines have divergent ultimate perspectives. However, they can be considered as examining the same phenomenon from different viewpoints.

Marketing science can be considered a branch of applied microeconomics, as it frequently utilizes choice modeling to analyze consumer behavior. This approach shares significant commonalities with the field of empirical industrial organization in economics. It is worth noting that recent developments in behavioral economics have led to the integration of psychological insights into mainstream economics. The same is true for marketing science. In the domain of agent-based computational economics, which emphasizes the bounded rationality of economic agents and social interactions, there have been a limited number of analogous initiatives in marketing science. However, several studies have employed agent-based modeling (ABM) as shown in this book.

As discussed in Chap. 1, the majority of research using ABM in marketing has focused on the diffusion of new products or the contagion of word-of-mouth communication related to product diffusion. In Chaps. 2, 3, and 4 of this book, we will introduce the simulations conducted by the author using ABM to study the diffusion of information on complex networks, building on the accumulated results of past research. From a marketing perspective, it is crucial to explore strategies that can accelerate the diffusion of new products. In this regard, the effectiveness of influencer marketing and seeding strategies will be examined as potential means to achieve this objective. It is noteworthy that numerous empirical studies have been conducted on this subject, underscoring the importance of identifying empirical rules based on data. However, it is equally essential to recognize the insights gained through simulations that show how simple microscopic actions can generate complex macroscopic behavior.

A prevalent criticism of ABM asserts that the model's assumptions and parameter settings are arbitrary, leading to unreliable results. While this concern may be seen as specific to ABM, it is important to note that this issue is not exclusive to ABM when viewed as a theoretical model. In the context of econometrics, it has become commonplace to estimate model parameters to ensure the model's fit with observed data. This approach is widely adopted, and it is reasonable to anticipate a similar development in ABM. In Chap. 5 of this book, the author presents his research endeavors aimed at enhancing the empirical validity of ABM inputs and outputs. It is acknowledged that this field is undergoing rapid evolution, and the methods discussed herein might not reflect the most recent advancements. Nevertheless, they could offer valuable insights into the challenges and the potential benefits of enhancing the empirical validity of ABM.

In Chap. 6, research that increases agent proactivity in ABM is presented. In models pertaining to the diffusion of new products, consumers' decision-making is predominantly influenced by external information and word-of-mouth recommendations from neighbors or peers. However, the processes captured by these models are characterized by a notable degree of passivity. This chapter delves into ABM, a model that acknowledges the potential for consumers to proactively enhance their own influence or monetize their influence. Specifically, we will introduce models where consumers seek influential positions and monetize their influence through affiliate marketing. We will conclude by pointing out that the influencer economy (or B2C2C economy), in which consumers are not just receivers but also strategic information senders, is an area that ABM will need to address in the future.

The research discussed in this book constitutes merely a fraction of the extant research on ABM in marketing science, and it is evident that there are numerous other excellent studies. Beyond the domain of marketing science, a considerable number of ABM studies developed in a wide range of fields, including economics, sociology, political science, computer science, and physics, have the potential to contribute to the understanding of marketing phenomena and the resolution of various problems. It is my hope that readers interested in the application of ABM to marketing, as fostered by this book, will direct their attention to these studies and embark on their own research in this domain.

In conclusion, I would like to express my profound appreciation to the Japan Association for Evolutionary Economics (JAFEE) for bestowing upon me the privilege to author this book. Additionally, I would like to express my profound gratitude to the co-authors of my own research presented in this book: Makoto Abe, Takayasu Baba, Naoki Shinbo, Shoichiro Inoue, Toshikatsu Mori, Naoki Nishiyama, Masami Noguchi, Hiroshi Onishi, Koto Sera, Satoru Shibuya, Yuto Takakai, and Hikaru Yamamoto. Additionally, I would like to express my sincere gratitude to Shota Hattori for introducing me to the intricacies of ABM, and to Eizo Akiyama for giving me the opportunity to attend the intensive lecture that forms the basis of this book. I am also indebted to the numerous researchers, both in Japan and abroad, who have provided invaluable comments and stimulation during academic conferences and research meetings.

Chiyoda-ku, Tokyo Makoto Mizuno

Contents

Chapter 1
Agent-Based Modeling for Marketing Science

This chapter provides an overview of the fundamental principles of agent-based modeling (ABM), with a particular emphasis on seminal works that have shaped the field. The initial focus is on two influential models: Schelling's segregation model [148] and Axelrod's cultural dissemination model [7, 8]. Furthermore, we examine the evolution of agents' decision-making rules through empirical learning, particularly referencing studies that integrate evolutionary algorithms with ABM [6, 123]. We conclude with a brief overview of the applications of ABM in marketing science.

1.1 Complex Systems and ABM

Agent-based modeling (ABM) is a widely utilized tool for the analysis of complex systems across a range of disciplines. In the 1980s, a group of distinguished researchers from diverse fields, including physics, computer science, life sciences, and economics, convened at the Santa Fe Institute in New Mexico, USA. They proposed the concept of complex systems, which they later expanded to encompass complex adaptive systems. In his recent comprehensive introduction, Hiroki Sayama defines these as follows:

> ... Complex systems are networks made of a number of components that interact with each other, typically in a nonlinear fashion. Complex systems may arise and evolve through self-organization, such that they are neither completely regular nor completely random, permitting the development of emergent behavior at macroscopic scales. ([147], p. 3)

This definition encompasses a wide range of phenomena, including both natural and socio-economic phenomena. In particular, the field of economics has been a significant area of research in the domain of complex systems since its inception. Prominent researchers such as Kenneth J. Arrow, a Nobel Prize-winning mathematical

M. Mizuno, *Complex Modeling of Consumer Behavior*, Evolutionary Economics and Social Complexity Science 34,
https://doi.org/10.1007/978-4-431-54874-4_1

economist, participated in early projects at the Santa Fe Institute [1]. John Casti, renowned for his insightful books on science, characterizes complex systems as follows:

> Typically, complex systems such as a stock market or a road-traffic network involve a medium-sized number of agents (traders or drivers) interacting on the basis of limited, partial information. And, most importantly, these agents are intelligent and adaptive. ([29], p. 11)

In this section, we will examine Casti's definition of complex systems, which reflects his critical stance toward conventional economic models. The focus on a medium-sized number of agents within the complex system distinguishes it from traditional mathematical economic models, such as game theory, which frequently concentrate on strategic interactions between a limited number of agents or, conversely, on an infinite market comprising a multitude of independent actors. The presence of a medium-sized number of agents gives rise to a greater degree of complexity in interactions, which in turn gives rise to heightened uncertainty. These systems are challenging to analyze using formal mathematical methods alone, necessitating computer simulations.

Furthermore, Casti highlights the limitations of the information available to agents, which contrasts with the assumptions made in traditional economic models that often presume high levels of rationality among agents. The incorporation of bounded rationality into mainstream economic frameworks through behavioral economics is a relatively recent development. However, the exploration of complex social interactions among agents remains largely underdeveloped, with the exception of agent-based computational economics. It is important to note, however, that Casti considers agents to be intelligent and adaptive, which contrasts with the holistic view of complex systems, where individual agent behavior is determined top-down by the system as a whole.

Agent-based modeling (ABM) is a research methodology that utilizes computational techniques to replicate and simulate complex systems, as previously outlined, using certain abstractions. Figure 1.1 provides an overview of the entire ABM system. The model consists of a finite number of agents who interact through a network and pursue individual goals based on the available information. As a result of these

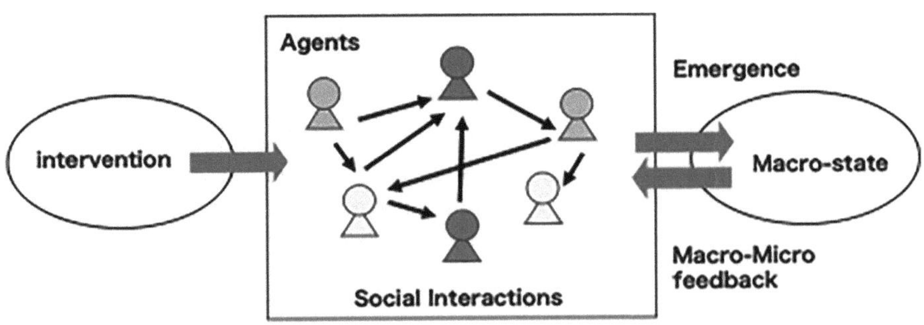

Fig. 1.1 Framework of agent-based modeling

interactions, patterns that are not evident at the micro level may emerge at the macro level—a phenomenon known as "emergence." The transfer of information from the macro state to individual agents is referred to as macro-micro feedback. In response, agents adjust their behavior, leading to dynamic changes in the entire system. When the research objective is to gain insights into system behavior, the challenge lies in simulating the outcomes of these changes. Alternatively, if the objective is to enhance outcomes, the challenge is to identify effective interventions.

In Casti's example of ABM applied to the financial market, the primary agents are traders who observe each other's behavior—sometimes through direct information exchange—to make decisions about buying and selling bonds. Consequently, bond prices are determined in the market, but unexpected nonlinear changes—such as price bubbles followed by sudden drops—can occur without many traders anticipating them. By developing an appropriate model of agent behavior and interactions, simulations can be conducted to explore strategies for market information feedback and agent behavior regulation. The goal is to prevent market instability.

This book primarily focuses on the application of ABM in marketing, where the typical agents are customers or, in some cases, companies (or brands). In consumer goods markets, the number of customers is substantial, and it was previously assumed that interactions among agents were negligible in marketing and economic models. However, this assumption is becoming increasingly untenable. The advent of social media has led to a significant shift in consumer interactions, making them more active than previously assumed. These interactions, which were once limited to homes, workplaces, schools, and local communities, have now expanded to a broader digital sphere. The impact of these interactions is often substantial and cannot be ignored (see, for example, [2]).

In markets where a monopoly or oligopoly of suppliers holds a dominant position, formal game theory can be effectively applied. In stable and mature markets, it is reasonable to assume that supply-side agents will choose near-optimal behavior based on the known demand function and anticipate their competitors' responses. However, in rapidly growing markets, the number of potential suppliers can be both unpredictable and vast. For example, in digital content markets, technological advancements have lowered entry barriers, enabling anyone to create and distribute content. In such markets, it is unclear who the competitors are and how they will act, forcing individual supply-side agents to adapt as best they can with limited information. Therefore, it is more appropriate to view the market as a complex system and employ ABM for analysis.

1.2 Classics of ABM in Social Science

This section presents and analyzes two classic agent-based modeling (ABM) models in social science. The first model, known as the "segregation model," was introduced by Thomas Schelling [148] to investigate the phenomenon of segregation in a metropolis where different racial or ethnic groups reside. In this model, agents

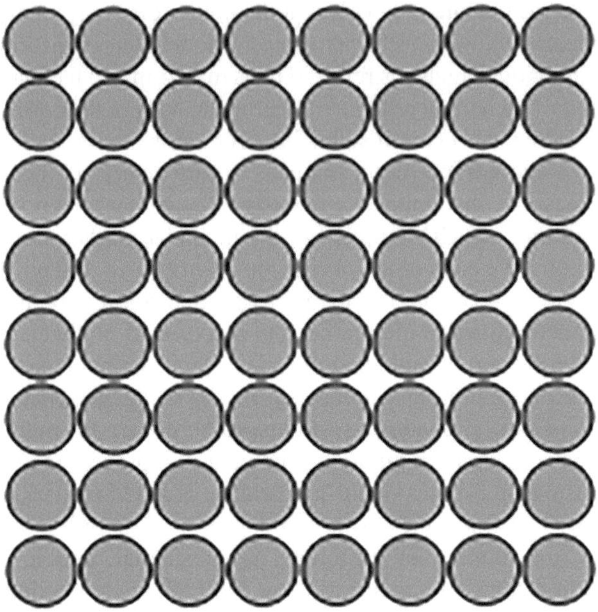

Fig. 1.2 Two-dimensional square lattice structure where agents are located

prefer to relocate when the proportion of individuals from different groups in their neighborhood exceeds a certain threshold. A key insight of the Schelling model is that segregation can occur even when individual preferences for same-group neighbors are relatively weak. The model represents agents living in a two-dimensional square lattice, where each square can accommodate a single agent, with some squares remaining empty. By simulating this model, it becomes evident that the distribution of resident types fluctuates and eventually reaches a state of equilibrium.

Another classic ABM study is Axelrod's cultural dissemination model [7, 8], which examines a two-dimensional square lattice where regions represent different cultures. Unlike Schelling's model, agents in this model represent regions and do not move. The culture of each agent evolves under the influence of neighboring agents. The cultural similarity between neighboring regions increases the likelihood of interaction. The model demonstrates that regions with similar cultures tend to become more homogeneous, while culturally diverse regions maintain their heterogeneity. Through repeated interactions, clusters of locally homogenized cultures emerge. The coexistence of these clusters suggests that cultural diversity may persist despite globalization.

Table 1.1 compares Schelling's segregation model and Axelrod's cultural dissemination model in terms of agent composition, agent decision-making, decision rule changes, agent networks, intervention strategies, and outcomes. Both models highlight how agent behavior can lead to bottom-up processes that form heterogeneous clusters or result in social fragmentation. These models serve as classic examples of ABM and offer valuable insights into understanding social phenomena.

Table 1.1 Comparison of two classic ABM studies

Characteristics	Segregation	Cultural dissemination
Agent composition	Residents of two races	Regions with different cultures
Agent decision	Stay where you are or move based on racial homogeneity	Imitate parts of their neighbors' culture based on cultural homogeneity
Rule change	None	None
Network	Square lattice	Square lattice (cyclic boundary)
Intervention	None	None
Outcome	Segregation by races	Stable diversity of cultures

The previously discussed models assume that agents' decision-making processes are simple, temporally fixed, and homogeneous. Considering the definition of complex systems presented in Sect. 1.1, it is reasonable to extend these models to incorporate evolving decision rules over time. One potential avenue for exploration is incorporating a natural selection mechanism, where decision rules undergo random changes through mutation and adapt in accordance with Darwinian evolutionary theory. An alternative approach is to introduce a learning mechanism, whereby agents learn from their own experiences or imitate others, as in Lamarckian evolutionary theory.

The model proposed by Nelson and Winter [123] integrates both approaches to model process innovation within an industry. In this model, the temporal state of each firm is represented by a vector of capital stocks and input-output coefficients, which are analogous to genes in organisms. These routines evolve through random mutation (Darwinian) and imitation (Lamarckian) and are "selected" through market competition. Simulations of the model demonstrate the persistence of intra-industry productivity dispersion as a macro state.

Another notable study that incorporates an evolutionary algorithm into ABM is Axelrod's repeated prisoner's dilemma tournament [6]. In this game, each player repeatedly faces the choice of cooperation or defection against other players. If both players keep choosing to cooperate, they can accumulate a sufficiently high payoff. On the other hand, if one player cooperates, the other can achieve a much higher payoff by defecting. Rational players are unlikely to sustain stable cooperation. However, experiments with such a game have shown that participants often choose to cooperate. The need to bridge this gap has inspired numerous studies, including Axelrod's tournament.

Axelrod organized a tournament in which multiple programmed strategies engaged in repeated iterations of the iterated prisoner's dilemma (IPD) game against different opponents. Researchers from around the world were invited to participate in this tournament. The participating strategies were randomly matched and played against each other on a computer. After a designated number of repetitions, the generation is updated. Strategies that perform better are replicated more frequently in the next generation, while those with inferior performance are eliminated. As time progresses, successful strategies are likely to face opponents of similar strength, including variations of themselves. Strategies that initially exploit weaker opponents may decline as fewer such opponents remain. Axelrod's simulations illustrate

Table 1.2 Comparison of two evolutionary ABMs

Characteristics	Nelson and Winter [123]	Axelrod [6]
Agent composition	Firms (producers)	Players for IPD games
Agent decision	Input-output coefficients	Cooperate or defect
Rule change	Random search, imitation	Generating offspring
Network	Complete network	Random network
Intervention	None	(Design of strategies)
Outcome	Distribution of productivity	Distribution of adaptive strategies

the high probability of survival for the Tit-for-Tat strategy, which defects if the opponent defects but cooperates if the opponent cooperates.[1]

Table 1.2 provides a comparative overview of the Nelson and Winter [123] and Axelrod [6] models within a unified framework, extending the insights presented in Table 1.1. The Nelson-Winter model, which posits that bounded-rational agents adapt to the market through trial and error, serves as an example of an agent-based model (ABM) as defined in the relevant literature. However, it does not incorporate local interactions among agents, as they merely imitate industry-wide best practices, resulting in a fully connected network. In contrast, the Axelrod tournament incorporates local interactions among agents, producing a network that resembles a random graph.

The application of evolutionary algorithms to updating game strategies has been extensively explored in the context of evolutionary game theory, with applications across a range of phenomena (see, for example, [22, 125]). In such games, the optimal strategy is not necessarily proactively chosen by forward-looking rational individuals. Instead, it emerges through competition among alternative conventions or heuristics (referred to as routines in the Nelson-Winter model), which each agent employs to achieve more favorable outcomes. If a strategy survives the competitive process and is replicated more frequently than others, it can be considered adaptively rational in the long run. Consequently, an ABM with an evolutionary algorithm serves as a tool for predicting the equilibrium or steady state that results from interactions among bounded-rational agents. If the objective of the study is to identify the strategies that emerge from prolonged interactions and agents' rule modifications, it is crucial that ABM incorporates evolutionary algorithms.

1.3 Studies Utilizing ABM in Marketing Science

Before examining the application of ABM in the study of marketing and consumer behavior, it is essential to provide a brief overview of marketing science. The field of marketing science originated in the 1960s [123]. Although academic research on marketing, including quantitative studies, had been conducted earlier, it was during

[1] It is important to note that there are criticisms regarding the generality of this conclusion [20, 139].

this period that the discipline was formally established as a branch of management science. From its inception, marketing science has drawn upon tools from operations research and management science, and later incorporated techniques from economics, psychology, statistics, and other disciplines.

ABM was likely added to the inventory of marketing science tools around the year 2000. It is my understanding that the first ABM paper published in a reputable international marketing journal was by Goldenberg et al. [64]. In their study, Goldenberg et al. [64] describe their methodology as cellular automata. A related article titled market percolation was published in a physics journal [67]. Both percolation and cellular automata can be considered forms of ABM implemented on a square lattice. Although numerous ABM studies have addressed marketing-related phenomena across various fields, including computer science, physics, and economics, our focus will be on marketing science journals and related disciplines to gain insight into how ABM is utilized in these domains.

Table 1.3 presents a list of journals from which the papers were collected. Initially, we included ten journals recognized among marketing science researchers, based on indicators such as impact factors and our own assessment. In addition, four management science journals that frequently publish marketing-related articles were also included. For each journal, papers containing the terms "agent-based model" or "agent-based modeling" in the title, abstract, or text were selected. Furthermore, papers that did not explicitly use these terms but clearly applied an approach analogous to agent-based modeling (ABM), based on our understanding, were also included. Conversely, papers that discussed the potential of ABM but did not include specific applied research were excluded from further analysis.

Table 1.3 Journals from which ABM studies were retrieved

		# articles
1	Industrial Marketing Review	1
2	International Journal of Research in Marketing	9
3	Journal of Academy of Marketing Science	0
4	Journal of Consumer Research	1
5	Journal of Marketing	3
6	Journal of Marketing Research	4
7	Journal of Retailing	1
8	Marketing Letters	2
9	Marketing Science	4
10	Quantitative Marketing and Economics	0
11	Journal of Business Research	11
12	Journal of Product Innovation Management	7
13	Management Science	2
14	Service Science	2

Note: # articles = the ones dealing with ABM in each journal between 2010 and 2022
It is worth noting that the high frequency of articles published in 2007 and 2011 is due to a special issue on ABM in some journals

Table 1.4 ABM studies in main marketing/management science journals

	Topic: Diffusion/WOM	Topic: Other marketing issues
2001	[64]	
2002	[65]	
2004	[54]	
2005	[55]	[156] [Competition]
2007	[39]; [42]; [56]; [63]; [166]	[83] [Competition]; [110] [Agenda]; [150] [Shopping]; [163] [Preference]; [173] [Preference]
2008	[136]	
2009	[62, 68]	[31] [Service]; [76] [B2B exchange]
2010	[21]; [36]; [43]; [66]	
2011	[24]; [137]; [165]; [171]; [172]	
2012	[46]	
2013	[74]; [102]; [162]	[32] [Service]
2014	[118]; [132]; [159]	
2015	[121]	[38] [Service]
2016	[41]; [48]; [122]; [154]	
2017	[35]; [44]	
2018	[80, 81]; [134]	
2022	[174]	

Note: The topics are listed in parentheses in the right column

Table 1.4 provides a chronological list of the selected papers. This list reveals that most Agent-Based Modeling (ABM) studies published in marketing or management science journals primarily focus on the diffusion of new products or innovations, emphasizing word-of-mouth propagation or various forms of interaction among potential adopters. However, some research, such as that by Watts and Dodds [166], emphasizes attitude change or opinion formation as a result of word-of-mouth propagation, rather than focusing on adoption or purchase. This mechanism is fundamentally similar to the diffusion model, as it addresses an irreversible binary state change. Chapter 2 will explore the contributions of diffusion models and ABM in marketing science.

1.4 Summary and Discussion

Agent-based modeling (ABM) has been employed across numerous disciplines as an effective tool for investigating complex systems. Its origins can be traced back to the study of cellular automata, which predates the emergence of the concept of complex systems. In addition to cellular automata, early applications of ABM in the social sciences were based on a square lattice, as exemplified by Schelling's segregation model [148] and Axelrod's cultural dissemination model [7, 8]. The square lattice assumption has been largely replaced as research on complex networks has advanced. With the accumulation of research on complex networks, ABM has evolved to incorporate heterogeneity in inter-agent relationships. Consequently, the ABM toolkit is becoming more comprehensive, facilitating the expansion of its applications.

The application of ABM in marketing science has primarily focused on the diffusion of new products. Casti [29] defined a complex adaptive system as one in which a medium-sized number of agents interact and adapt to their environment based on limited information. In marketing, one phenomenon that exemplifies this definition is the diffusion process of a new product. The greater the degree of innovation associated with a new product, the less certain potential adopters are about its value, and the more susceptible they are to the influence of word-of-mouth information. However, it is important to note that ABM has been applied to marketing topics beyond the diffusion of new products, albeit in limited numbers. Exploring new potential applications of ABM would be beneficial, as the complex interactions between consumers and between consumers and firms are likely to play an increasingly important role in marketing in the future.

Another promising avenue for the application of ABM is in cases where agents do not act in a manner that can be considered rational, or where the consequences differ from their expectations, even if they are subjectively rational. In such cases, incorporating an evolutionary algorithm into ABM is an effective approach, allowing agents' behavioral rules to evolve through a process of "natural selection." Pioneering studies of the evolutionary approach include Nelson and Winter's model of innovation [123] and Axelrod's prisoner's dilemma tournaments [6].

An extension of this line of research can be observed in the emergence of evolutionary economics and agent-based computational economics [157]. However, there is a lack of existing research in this area within marketing science. One reason for this is that the marketing science perspective is often not long-term enough to accommodate the evolutionary analogy. Nevertheless, applying ABM to macroscopic strategic issues related to product life cycles or sustainable competitive advantages may prove beneficial. It is hoped that breakthroughs will soon be made in applying ABM to marketing.

Chapter 2
New Production Diffusion and ABM

The diffusion of new products has been a central topic in agent-based modeling (ABM) within marketing science. The Bass model [13] serves as a foundational framework for diffusion models in this field [119, 131]. Following the tradition of the Bass model, the agent-based diffusion modeling approach developed by Goldenberg et al. [64] made a significant initial contribution to the field. In this book, it will henceforth be referred to as the GLM model. This chapter provides an overview of these models and discusses their extensions, with a particular focus on incorporating complex network structures.

2.1 Traditional Diffusion Model in Marketing

The diffusion of a new product can be conceptualized as the cumulative process of individual adoptions in the market. Rogers' seminal work on the diffusion of innovations has significantly influenced both marketing theory and practice [141]. His research covers a range of innovations beyond consumer marketing, including advancements in agriculture and medicine. Rogers' framework, which categorizes adopters into five groups innovators, early adopters, early majority, late majority, and laggards—remains a cornerstone of diffusion studies. However, Rogers' descriptive approach, which lacked formal models, limited the utility of his work for quantitative analysis. In response to this limitation, Bass [13] developed a pioneering quantitative model.

Before examining the Bass model, it is essential to identify the types of data fundamental to the study of new product diffusion. Typically, diffusion is measured by aggregating the number of individual product adoptions. As new product adoption corresponds to an initial purchase, repurchases should not be counted as new adoptions. Panel data that track individual purchase histories enable the

M. Mizuno, *Complex Modeling of Consumer Behavior*, Evolutionary Economics and Social Complexity Science 34,
https://doi.org/10.1007/978-4-431-54874-4_2

differentiation between initial purchases and repurchases. In contrast, purchase data observed over time without continuity at the individual level fails to provide this distinction.[1]

Digital content distributed via the Internet is particularly well-suited for diffusion models, as it is typically downloaded only once and consumed over time. Similarly, the number of times a film is viewed can be effectively modeled, given that audiences typically attend theaters only once for a specific film. However, for frequently purchased consumer goods such as food and toiletries, initial purchases may indicate a trial rather than a genuine adoption. This distinction partially explains the limited applicability of diffusion models, such as the Bass model, to such goods.

Diffusion models, such as the Bass model, propose that the adoption of a new product signifies an irreversible transition from the state of non-adoption (0) to the state of adoption (1) at the individual level. Consequently, the diffusion or penetration rate, representing the aggregated individual adoptions over time, follows a monotonically increasing trend. Panel data can be employed to accurately capture this irreversible change. However, independently collected diffusion data at different time points may show a decreasing trend due to sampling errors or population changes.

Muller [119] provides a comprehensive overview of diffusion research history in marketing science, emphasizing the central role of the Bass model. The model suggests that potential adopters can be divided into two latent segments: innovators and imitators. Let us denote the coefficients of external factor (innovation) and internal factor (imitation) by p and q, respectively. If the cumulative number of adopters of a new product at time t is denoted as $X(t)$, its increment is formulated as follows:

$$dX(t)/dt = \left(p + q\frac{X(t)}{m}\right)(m - X(t)) \tag{2.1}$$

where m denotes the total number of potential adopters. This model postulates that the probability of adoption at time t is influenced by both internal and external factors. When data are available, external factors, such as advertising, can be incorporated into the model as exogenous variables.

One of the key advantages of the Bass model is its flexibility, as illustrated in Fig. 2.1. It can represent both the S-shaped diffusion pattern observed in logistic curves and the rapid growth seen in modified exponential curves. As such, the Bass model has become a standard for new product diffusion modeling, inspiring extensive subsequent research in marketing science.

A limitation of the Bass model is its assumption that the number of potential adopters remains fixed at m. However, in reality, the composition of potential adopters may change, and the diffusion rate may not always follow a strictly increasing

[1] In cases where the data do not allow for the differentiation between initial purchases and subsequent repurchases, the analysis of the diffusion model may exclude periods during which repurchases predominate. In such instances, the impact of individual differences in purchase intervals is disregarded.

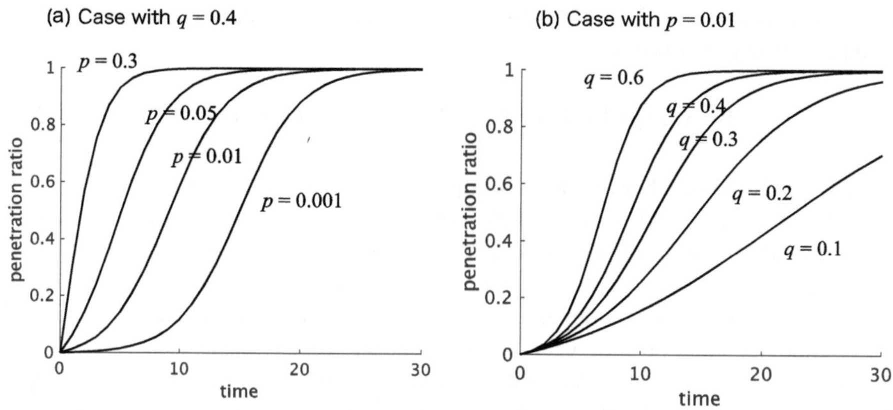

Fig. 2.1 Diffusion curves of the Bass model with varying parameters

trend. Factors such as aging or migration can lead to potential adopters entering or exiting the population, resulting in variations in the number of adopters. Fixing the population is generally an acceptable simplification, but in some cases, changes in the population should be considered, especially in long-term diffusion studies. If the data show a temporary decrease in the number of adopters, it is often treated as noise; however, this approach is not always appropriate.

Muller [119] classifies the initial extensions of the Bass model into four primary categories: (1) successive generations, (2) incorporation of decision variables, (3) international comparisons, and (4) brand-driven growth. The availability of substantial data on individual purchasing behaviors has led subsequent studies to utilize hazard models for predicting the timing of adoption. Furthermore, in recent years, there has been growing interest in incorporating social interactions among consumers into diffusion models, which has led to the advent of ABM.

2.2 Agent-Based Diffusion Model in Marketing

The GLM model [64] represents a significant advancement of diffusion models based on agent-based modeling [119, 131], following the tradition of the Bass model [13]. This section reviews the GLM model and its extensions, with a particular emphasis on the 2010 extension that incorporates a threshold-based pre-screening decision stage in the adoption process [66].

2.2.1 Basic Goldenberg-Libai-Muller (GLM) Model

The GLM model posits that the adoption of new products is influenced by a combination of external and internal factors, denoted by π and θ, respectively. Let $x_h(t)$ be a dummy variable that takes the value of 1 if agent h (=1, 2, …, m) adopts a new product at time t (= 1, 2, ..., T). This model formulates an individual agent's adoption probability as follows:

$$\Pr\left[x_h(t)=1|x_h(\tau)=0,\tau<0\right]=1-(1-\pi)(1-\theta)^{n_h(t-1)} \tag{2.2}$$

where $n_h(t)$ is the number of adopters adjacent to agent h at time t.

In the original GLM model, agents are divided into distinct communities with complete intra-community networks and partial inter-community connections. This structure reflects the concepts of strong and weak ties, as proposed by Granovetter [73]. The diffusion process depends on weak ties, as individuals who are contacted less frequently often provide valuable information [17, 26, 47, 61].

Goldenberg et al. [65] observed a saddle-shaped sales trajectory for multiple durable consumer goods, characterized by an initial stagnation followed by growth. They attributed this pattern to the differential impact of internal and external factors in early and main markets, aligning with the chasm theory [117]. Model simulations provided insights into the conditions that lead to such diffusion patterns.

2.2.2 *GLM Model with a Pre-screening Decision Stage*

Goldenberg et al. [66] introduced the concept of network externalities, whereby the benefits of adoption depend on the number or percentage of network members. This model incorporates a two-stage decision-making process. In the initial stage, each potential adopter conducts a pre-screening of adoption prospects based on whether the market-wide diffusion rate exceeds their specified threshold. If the pre-screening criteria are met, the individual proceeds to the second decision stage, which is driven by a combination of external and internal factors, as illustrated in the GLM model.

The modified adoption probability is:

$$\begin{aligned}\Pr\left[x_h(t)=1|x_h(\tau)=0,\tau<0\right]&=1-(1-\pi)(1-\theta)^{n_h(t-1)},\ if\ \frac{n(t-1)}{m}>\gamma_h\\&=0,\text{else}\end{aligned} \tag{2.3}$$

where $n(t)$ is the number of adopters in the entire market at time t, and g_h is the threshold in pre-screening for agent h.

The threshold is assumed to vary across individuals according to a normal distribution with mean μ and variance σ^2, being constant over time. That is, the distribution of the threshold is written as follows:

$$g_h \sim N(\mu,\sigma^2) \tag{2.4}$$

Potential adopters with lower thresholds proceed directly to the final decision stage, which is analogous to the basic GLM model. In contrast, those with higher thresholds delay transitioning to the second stage until the market-wide diffusion rate exceeds their threshold. Figure 2.2a illustrates the adoption probability in response to the number of network neighbors in the GLM model, demonstrating a concave response function. The introduction of a threshold at the pre-screening decision stage, under specific conditions, transforms the overall response function into an S-shaped curve, as shown in Fig. 2.2b. In the scenario where the threshold is present but its mean is set to zero, the overall response function tends to follow an S-shaped pattern, as depicted in Fig. 2.2a.

Goldenberg et al. [66] evaluate the overall performance of a given diffusion process in terms of NPV (Net Present Value), which is defined as the sum of the present value of temporal revenues, discounted at a rate of d. The temporal revenue is calculated by multiplying the incremental number of adopters at time t, represented by $\Delta X(t)$, assuming that the average revenue per adopter is fixed at 1 for simplicity. The equation for this calculation is:

$$\mathrm{NPV} = \sum_{t=1}^{T} \Delta X(t) / (1+d)^{t-1} \tag{2.5}$$

Since NPV is a single metric, it serves as an expedient means of evaluating disparate diffusion patterns. An alternative approach would be to utilize the diffusion rate for each period; however, this requires identifying the most critical point in time. In practice, the diffusion rate at a given point in time may be identical, while diffusion trajectories may vary. NPV integrates profits over the entire period, ensuring the inclusion of all relevant data. The calculation of NPV requires determining a discount rate, a process that is relatively straightforward for practitioners. Consequently, the evaluation of diffusion studies in marketing frequently employs NPV as a key indicator.

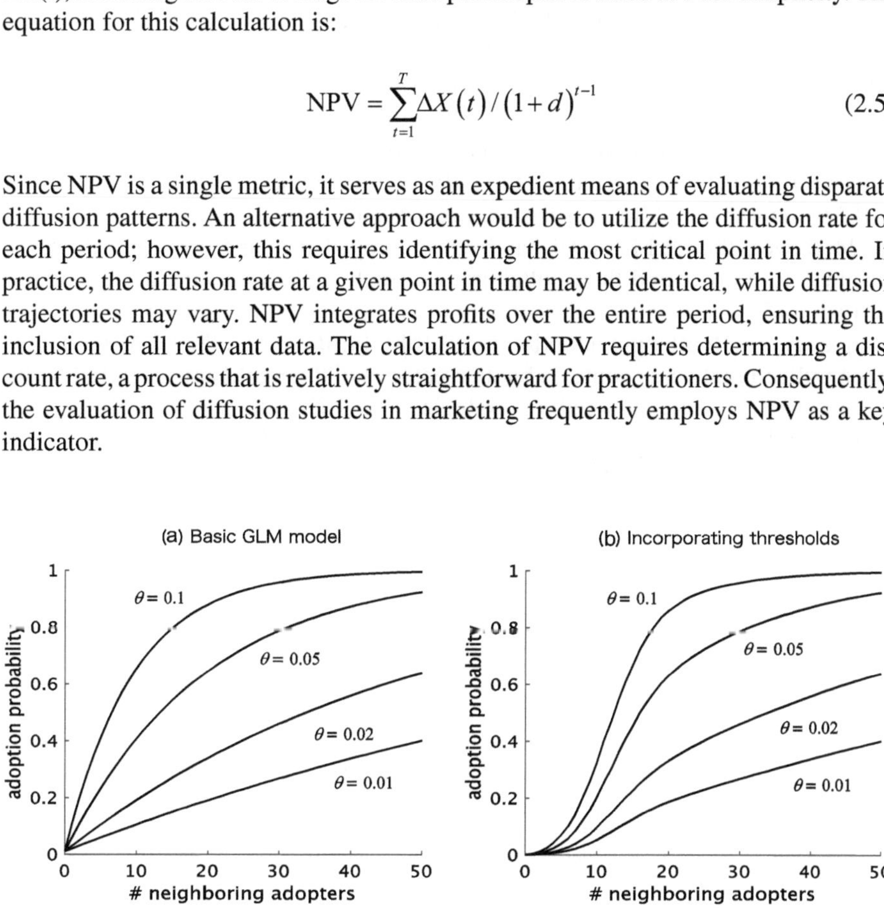

Fig. 2.2 Responses of adoption probability to the number of neighboring adopters. Note: Fig. 2.2b represents the adoption probability response to the number of neighboring adopters, assuming that each node connects to 50 nodes, global and local diffusion rates coincide, and the threshold distribution follows $N(0.2, 0.1)$

Goldenberg et al. [66] examine the existence of the "chilling effect" of network externalities on new product diffusion. The magnitude of this effect is quantified as the ratio of NPV with the externality to NPV without it: the larger the chilling effect, the smaller the ratio. Simulation results indicate that the chilling effect is amplified when individual variations in thresholds are small relative to the mean. The existence of this effect is further supported by empirical analysis using an aggregate-level model based on real market data.

2.2.3 Further Extensions of the GLM Model

In the study by Goldenberg et al. [66], potential adopters are represented as interlinked agents within a square lattice structure (Table 2.1). Modifying this agent interconnection with a more complex network may produce different results. Mukherjee [118] conducted simulations of the aforementioned model using empirical network data from various sources. The findings generally confirm the chilling effects of network externalities, although there are a few exceptions. Specifically, under certain network structures, the NPV with network externalities exceeds the NPV without them, although such occurrences are relatively rare.

Moreover, the GLM model has been employed in numerous contexts by its original developers and their collaborators. Such applications include geospatial diffusion [54], negative word-of-mouth effects [63], and markets exhibiting high frequency and fluctuating adoption ratios [68]. Furthermore, the GLM model has been utilized in diverse contexts by its creators and their colleagues, including the development of efficient seeding strategies [74, 102], integration with the Bass model and penetration rate prediction [159], and other applications. Other researchers have also adopted the GLM model as a component of the diffusion

Table 2.1 Comparison of extended GLM models

	GLM (2001) [64]	GLM (2002) [65]	GLM (2010) [66]
Agent composition	Potential adopters	Potential adopters, of initial/main market	Potential adopters
Agent decision	Adopt the new product or not, by the influence of neighboring adopters	Adopt or not, by the influence of neighboring or early market adopters	Adopt or not, by the effect of network externalities and the influence of neighboring adopters
Rule change	None	None	None
Network	Multiple partially connected complete networks	Two partially connected square lattices	Square lattice
Intervention	None	None	(Remove of a network externality)
Outcome	Information dissemination	Depth and width of saddle	NPV impact of externalities

model [121, 122]. Despite the existence of other agent-based diffusion model formulations, the GLM model has indisputably given rise to the most fruitful research endeavors.

2.3 Incorporation of Complex Networks

Let us consider the type of network structure and the manner of its incorporation into the GLM model. Theoretically, regular and random networks are relatively simple. However, in the study of complex networks, small-world networks and scale-free networks have become known as network structures with more realistic properties. These more complex networks can be generated as derivatives from regular networks. Therefore, the generation of these network structures is discussed below. The network corresponding to the original GLM is a set of several complete networks that are partially interconnected, which is somewhat unique and not included in this discussion.

2.3.1 Theoretically Abstract Networks as a Basis

The majority of traditional ABMs are based on simplified square lattice structures. When periodic boundary conditions are satisfied, the corresponding network becomes a regular network in which all nodes exhibit the same number of links. Another theoretical network structure is the random network, where the probability of a link existing between any pair of nodes remains constant. It is evident that these network structures diverge significantly from the structural characteristics observed in real-world social networks. However, it is important to acknowledge that they serve as the foundation for extensive theoretical inquiry.

Consequently, the regular network is used as a foundation to generate networks with more realistic properties, such as those observed in small-world or scale-free networks. Figure 2.3 illustrates an example of a regular network—a connected network in which all nodes have four links (i.e., each node's degree is four). The network is generated by arranging all nodes in a circle and establishing links between each node and its neighboring nodes, including one additional neighbor. The specific generation techniques will be explained in the following subsections.

2.3.2 Generating Small-World or Purely Random Networks

Watts and Strogatz [167] introduced the concept of small-world networks, a type of complex network that more accurately reflects certain aspects of real social network structures. The defining characteristic of small-world networks is the existence of

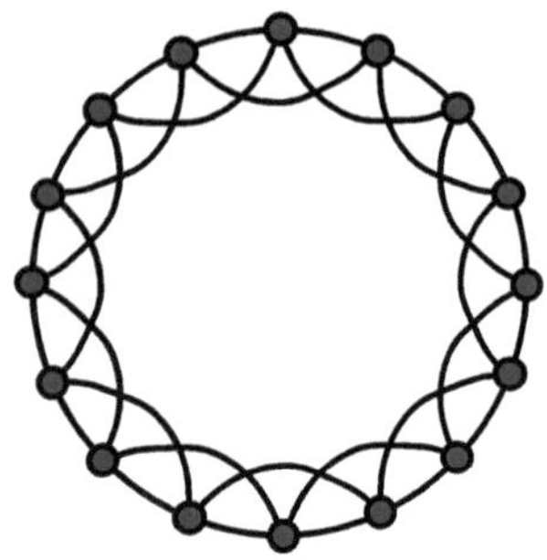

Fig. 2.3 An illustrative regular network

Table 2.2 Properties of algorithmically generated networks

Network	Rewiring probability	# iterations	Average distance	Clustering coefficient	Network structure
G0	0.0	1	125.3	0.50	Regular
G1	0.1	1	11.7	0.42	
G2	0.2	1	9.0	0.38	Small-world
G3	0.3	1	7.4	0.30	Small-world
G4	0.5	1	6.4	0.20	Small-world
G5	0.7	1	6.0	0.13	
G6	1.0	1	5.6	0.06	Purely random

relatively short average distances between nodes despite the presence of high average clustering coefficients, given a limited number of links.[2] The relatively short average distances within the network facilitate the rapid propagation of information, while a high average clustering coefficient indicates that two nodes connected to a specific node are likely to be interconnected.

Furthermore, they proposed an algorithm for generating small-world networks. In the following analysis, the algorithm is applied to a regular network comprising 1000 nodes, each with a degree of four. Table 2.2 illustrates the impact of varying rewiring probabilities on the average distance and clustering coefficient. The rows, designated G0, G1, …, G6, correspond to different values of the probability. This indicates a nonlinear transition even with a relatively low rewiring probability, significantly reducing the average distance while maintaining a relatively stable average clustering coefficient. Therefore, it is suggested that the transition to small-world networks begins around G2.

As the probability of rewiring approaches one, the network transitions into a purely random network, thereby losing its small-world properties. Figures 2.4 and 2.5 present plots of these networks and their respective degree distributions. The

[2] The distance between nodes in a network is defined as the shortest path between two nodes. The mean distance is the average of the shortest paths between all possible pairs of nodes. In contrast, the average clustering coefficient represents the probability that two randomly selected nodes, both of which are connected to a common node, are also connected to each other [167].

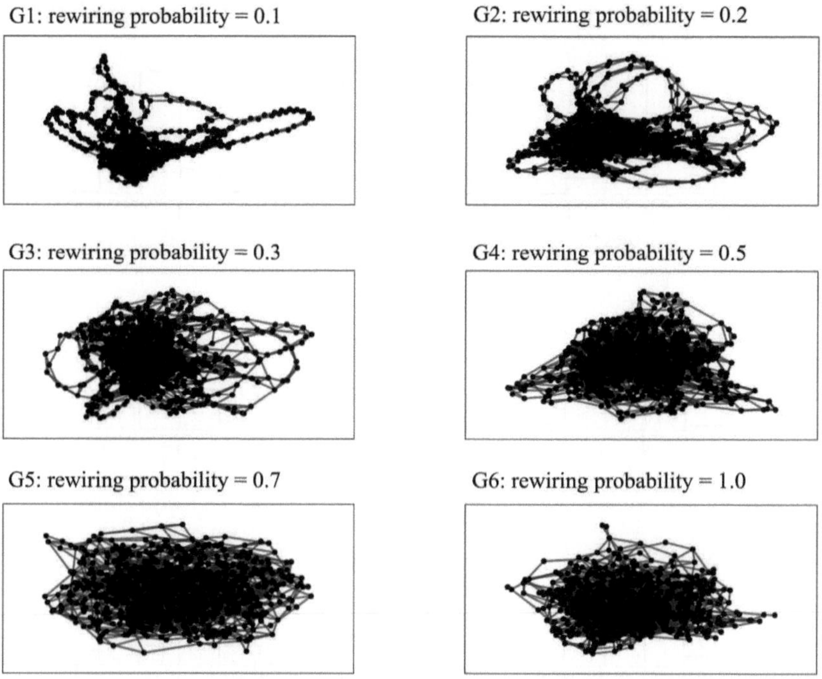

Fig. 2.4 Plots of small-world/purely random networks

degree distributions for all networks are approximately symmetric around four, and the variances increase as the rewiring probability rises. As a result, it is not possible to distinguish between small-world and purely random networks based solely on these figures. Instead, careful reference to the average distance and clustering coefficients is required to make a determination. However, even then, no significant threshold exists, and they can only be interpreted as relative differences.

2.3.3 Generating Near Scale-Free Networks

The degree distribution of a network, which denotes the bias in links between nodes, is of paramount importance for identifying networks that exhibit characteristics distinct from those of small-world networks. An analysis of the degree distributions of real-world networks has revealed the existence of networks with a small number of nodes exhibiting exceedingly high degrees [11]. In such cases, the degree distribution demonstrates a substantial long-tail pattern. A prime example is the Twitter user network, where many accounts have few followers, while a small number of accounts have millions of followers [94]. When the degree distribution follows a power-law pattern, the network is classified as a scale-free network. Nodes with

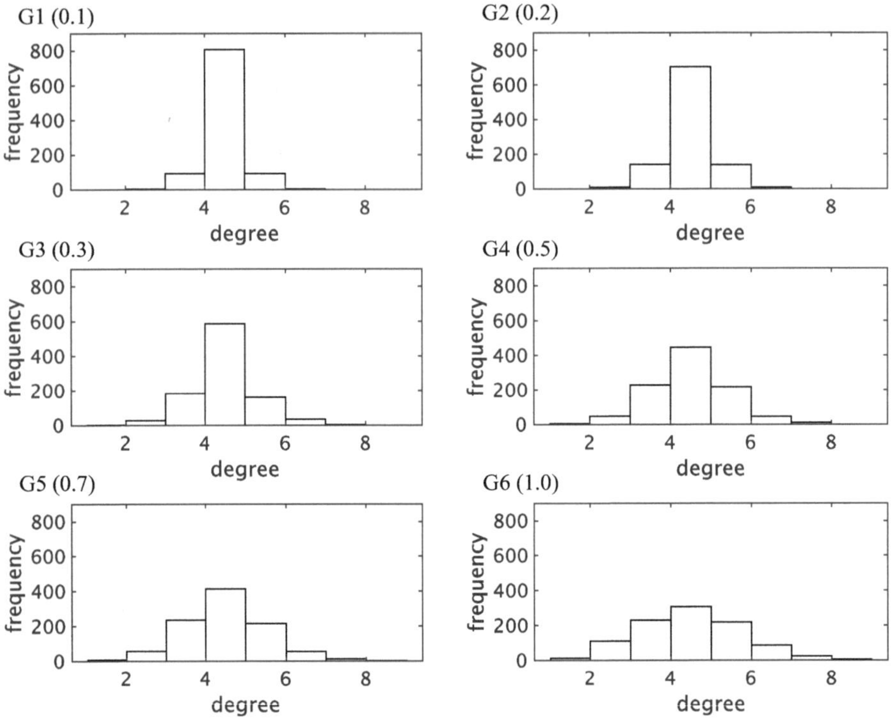

Fig. 2.5 Degree distributions of small-world/purely random networks. Note: The figures in parentheses represent the probability of rewiring

higher degrees, known as hubs, are often key targets for word-of-mouth (WOM) marketing.

Scale-free networks are generated by rewiring links in a regular network, employing the "preferential attachment" principle initially proposed by Barabási and Albert [12]. This principle prioritizes nodes with higher degrees, thereby increasing the likelihood of such nodes being selected as link destinations. The rewiring probability is set to 0.5, and the process is iterated a predetermined number of times. Figure 2.6 illustrates networks generated with varying numbers of iterations. The differences in their properties are not readily apparent from visual inspection alone; therefore, a comparative analysis of their average distances and clustering coefficients (Table 2.3), as well as their degree distributions (Fig. 2.7), is essential.

As the number of iterations increases, the degree distribution initially resembles a log-normal distribution (G8) but gradually approaches a power-law distribution (G9, G10). By fitting a linear regression model to the log-transformed values of both the degrees and their frequencies, the power exponent can be estimated, indicating whether the degree distribution follows a power-law pattern. As illustrated in Fig. 2.8 and Table 2.4, networks G9 and G10 can be classified as quasi-scale-free networks, given the slight inadequacy of the regression model in fitting the data, even after 10 to 20 iterations.

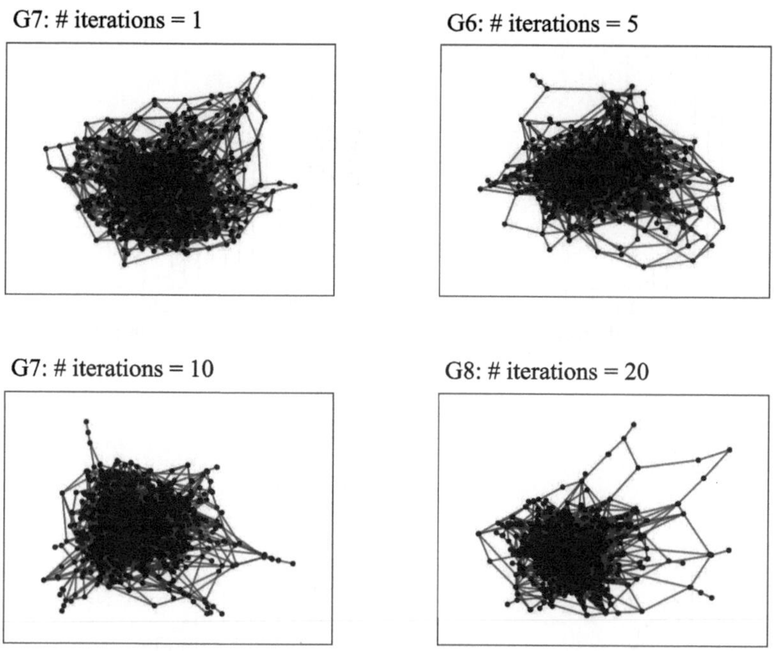

Fig. 2.6 Plots of quasi scale-free networks with a rewiring probability of 0.5

Table 2.3 Properties of algorithmically generated networks

Network	Rewiring probability	Number of iterations	Average distance	Clustering coefficient	Network structure
G7	0.5	2	5.6	0.09	
G8	0.5	5	5.1	0.01	Random with hubs[a]
G9	0.5	10	4.8	0.01	Quasi scale-free
G10	0.5	20	4.7	0.01	Quasi scale-free

[a] The degree distribution of the network is nearly log-normal, whereas it is nearly power-law in quasi scale-free networks

2.3.4 Networks in Agent-Based Diffusion Models

The advancement of complex network studies has significantly impacted the investigation of agent-based diffusion models, as evidenced by the findings presented in Table 2.5. Initial research in this field focused on incorporating small-world networks into these models (see [36, 54, 63, 134, 166]). Subsequently,

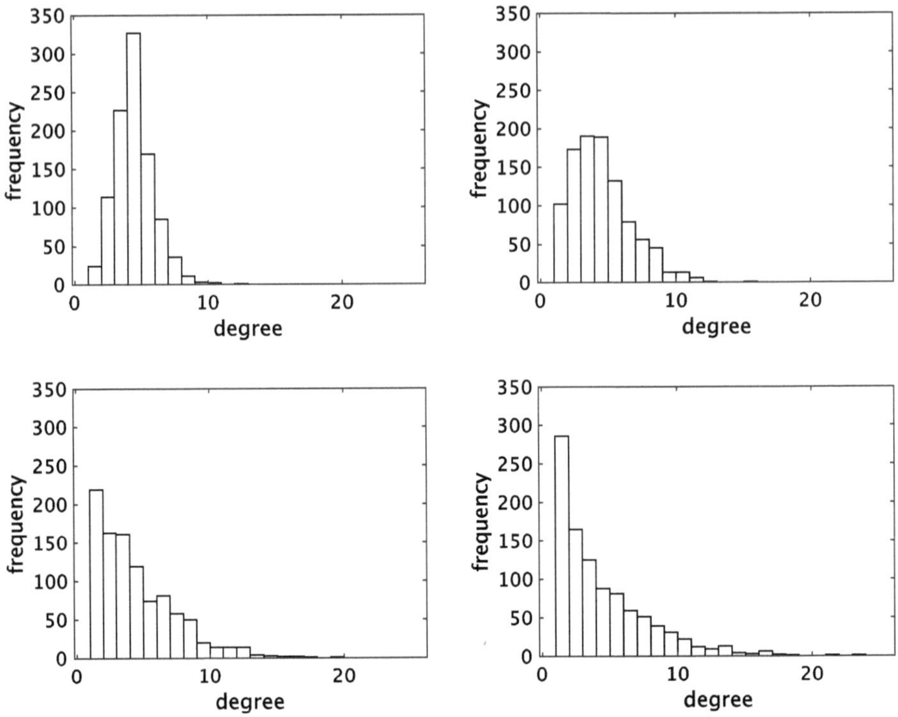

Fig. 2.7 Degree distributions of quasi-scale-free networks with a rewiring probability of 0.5

studies were conducted that integrated scale-free networks [45, 154]. Some studies have combined these two representative complex networks ([21, 46, 48, 162]).

It should be noted that both small-world and scale-free networks are artificially generated through algorithms and do not perfectly replicate real-world networks. Consequently, some studies utilize empirically observed networks from various domains (e.g., cell phone call networks) and simulate agent behaviors within them [36, 74, 102, 118, 121, 122, 132, 162]. Although this research approach holds considerable promise, it is important to note that a significant proportion of the network data has been collected independently of the target market for each study. To gain a deeper understanding of the impact of generalized network properties on diffusion performance, it may be more practical to conduct simulations on algorithmically generated networks.[3]

[3] A comprehensive review of the contributions of social network and complex network research to agent-based diffusion models can be found in Muller and Peres [120] or Rand and Stummer [138].

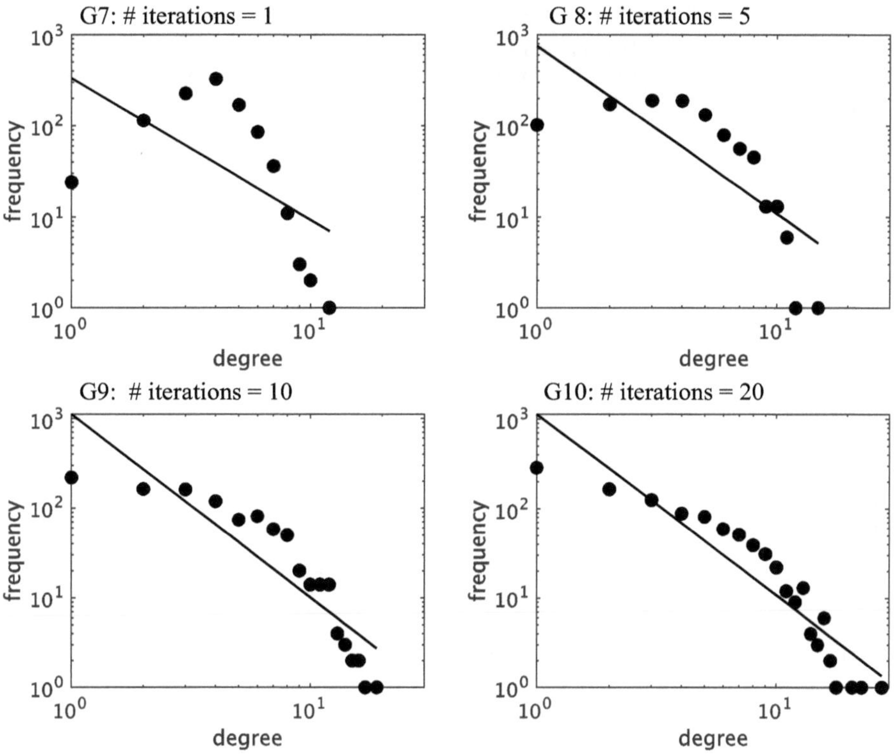

Fig. 2.8 Log-log plot of degree distributions in Fig. 2.7 and the regression lines

Table 2.4 Result of linear regression on degree distributions

Network	Rewiring probability	Number of iterations	Power exponent	s.e.	sig.	R^2
G7	0.5	2	1.556	0.727	c	0.338
G8	0.5	5	1.841	0.467	s	0.585
G9	0.5	10	2.042	0.263	s	0.790
G10	0.5	20	2.021	0.190	s	0.856

Note: Columns "s.e." and "sig." indicate the standard error of the estimated power exponent and its statistical significance, respectively: s: $p < .001$; c: $p < .10$, with 21 observations

2.4 Summary and Discussion

The GLM agent-based diffusion model [64] is based on a theoretical shift from the Bass model. Both models typically posit that the adoption of new products is driven by an interplay of external and internal factors. However, a distinctive feature of the GLM model, as well as numerous other agent-based diffusion models, is the explicit incorporation of network structure among potential adopters. It is, therefore, of

Table 2.5 Network structures used in agent-based diffusion models

	Network structure					
	RG	RN	SW	SF	PC	RW
[64]					x	
[65]	x					
[54]			x			
[63]			x			
[166]			x			
[62], [68]					x	
[21]	x	x	x	x		
[36]			x			
[66]	x					
[137]		x		x		
[46]			x	x		
[102]						x
[74]						x
[162]			x	x		x
[118]	x					x
[132]						x
[121]						x
[41]				x		
[48]			x	x		
[122]						x
[154]				x		
[35]						x
[134]			x			

Note: RG: Regular networks; RN: Random networks; SW: Small-world networks; SF: Scale-free networks; PC: Partially connected multiple complete networks; RW: Real-world networks

paramount importance to determine which network structure should be incorporated into the model.

One avenue for further development of the GLM model is the incorporation of empirically observed networks. This approach has already been applied to the GLM model, as evidenced by the work of Mukherjee [118] and Libai et al. [102]. However, it should be noted that these networks were archived and, therefore, may not be directly relevant to the adoption behavior under analysis. While it would be optimal to observe both networks and adoption behavior from the same subjects, this is often challenging in practice. In the absence of data from the same subjects, Chaps. 2, 3, 4, 5 of this book primarily utilize synthetically generated networks based on complex network research. Although this approach is not empirically validated, it provides theoretical insights. However, the network structures under comparison are relatively simple, and extending them to more closely resemble real-world networks remains a challenge for future research.

An additional avenue for extending the GLM model is examining the complexity of new product adoption behavior. Goldenberg et al. [66] developed a two-stage process to describe this phenomenon. Although this extension may increase the model's complexity, it offers the advantage of expanding the range of phenomena that can be analyzed. One of the most significant advantages is the ability to accommodate S-shaped diffusion curves, which have been regarded as the gold standard in diffusion research, within the context of an agent-based diffusion model. The greater the novelty associated with a new product, the longer it will take to penetrate the market. The incorporation of a pre-screening stage into the overall adoption process allows for the examination of various diffusion trajectory patterns.

The integration of threshold-based pre-screening into the two-stage decision-making process is also observed in the field of behavioral decision research. It is argued that as the number of alternatives and their attributes increases, the cognitive cost to the decision-maker also increases, leading to the use of heuristics [128]. The cognitive costs associated with new product adoption differ from those arising from a lack of knowledge about attributes and uncertainty regarding quality. Further empirical research is required to determine which heuristics are employed in such cases.

Chapter 3
Simulation of an Agent-Based Diffusion Model

This chapter analyzes the agent-based diffusion model introduced in the previous chapter, with a particular focus on how it produces varying diffusion outcomes. The model has two distinctive features: the incorporation of a network structure among potential adopters and a two-stage adoption decision process, which consists of pre-screening and final adoption decisions. These features result in diverse diffusion patterns depending on the network structure. The simulation results are examined using two approaches. First, diffusion trajectories are visualized to illustrate the impact of different conditions, such as network structure and agents' behavioral parameters. Second, the diffusion outcomes are aggregated into an index, Net Present Value (NPV), and regression analyses are conducted to statistically evaluate the effects of simulation conditions.

3.1 Model Specification and Parameter Setting

As previously outlined, the agent-based diffusion model proposed by Goldenberg et al. [66] incorporates a pre-screening decision with reference to market-wide diffusion rates as a precursor to adoption decisions driven by external and internal factors, following a tradition established by Bass [13]. This study further extends the aforementioned model by assuming that pre-screening is not only reliant on global reference groups but also on local reference groups. Local reference groups can be defined as a set of neighbors who are directly linked via a network. A model in which the diffusion rate within such a reference group is critical has been proposed by Watts and Dodds [166] and others.

One might inquire as to why the diffusion rate within reference groups affects the adoption of new products at the pre-screening stage. Goldenberg et al. [66] assumed that network externalities function prior to the adoption decision-making process. It

M. Mizuno, *Complex Modeling of Consumer Behavior*, Evolutionary Economics and Social Complexity Science 34,
https://doi.org/10.1007/978-4-431-54874-4_3

should be noted, however, that there are other potential mechanisms through which market-wide or network-local neighborhood diffusion rates may impact new product adoption. These will be discussed in Sect. 3.4, as they are unlikely to directly influence the formulation of the model presented here.

The following three scenarios are considered in relation to the decisions of agents who may potentially adopt the proposed approach. In the first scenario, the pre-screening decision stage is effectively eliminated, resulting in a model that is essentially identical to that proposed by Goldenberg et al. [64]. In the second scenario, the reference groups are global, and the pre-screening decision is made based on the market-wide diffusion rate (the case of global references), which aligns with the study conducted by Goldenberg et al. [66]. Each agent's adoption model for this scenario is in Eq. 2.3 of Chap. 2. In the third scenario, agents utilize the diffusion rate of their network neighbors for pre-screening, which is representative of local references. For the third scenario, the adoption model is rewritten as follows:

$$\begin{aligned} \Pr\left[x_h(t)=1 \middle| x_h(\tau)=0, \tau<0\right] &= 1-(1-\pi)(1-\theta)^{n_h(t-1)}, \ if \ \frac{n_h(t-1)}{m_h} > \gamma_h \\ &= 0, \text{else} \end{aligned} \tag{3.1}$$

where

$x_h(t) = 1$ if agent h adopts the new product at time t, otherwise $x_h(t) = 0$,

π: The probability that an agent adopts due to the external factor,

θ: The probability that an agent adopts due to the internal factor, which is the influence of adjacent adopters (agents who already adopted) on the network,

$n_h(t)$: The number of adopters adjacent to agent h on the network at time t,

m_h: The number of agents in agent h's reference group,

$g_h \sim N(\mu, \sigma^2)$: The threshold at the pre-screening stage for agent h.

The simulation conditions are defined as follows: The number of agents, M, representing potential adopters of a new product, is set at 1000. The agents are connected through a single undirected network, comprising a total of 2000 links between agents, resulting in an average node degree of 4. The predetermined conditions for the pre-screening decision stage include the values of the threshold mean (μ) and standard deviation (σ), as well as whether reference groups are local or global. If the mean value, μ, is equal to zero, then half of the potential adopters do not engage in threshold-based pre-screening, which is classified as a "weak screening" scenario. Conversely, if the mean value, μ, is significantly greater than zero, these cases are classified as "strong screening" scenarios. The conditions for the final adoption decision stage are defined by the external factor (π) and the internal factor (θ).

As illustrated in Table 3.1, two options were designated for each of the conditions, with the exception of those pertaining to network structures. The specific values for each option were selected based on preliminary simulations to ensure that a plausible range of diffusion curves could be achieved. Six network structures (G0, G2, G4, G6, G8, G10) were selected from the algorithm-generated networks detailed

Table 3.1 Alternative simulation conditions

		Level 1	Level 2
Adoption	External factor (π)	0.001	0.01
	Internal factor (θ)	0.05	0.10
Pre-screening	Mean of thresholds (μ)	0.00	0.10
	Standard deviation of thresholds (σ)	0.05	0.10
	Reference group (ref)	Local	Global
Network	Regular (G0), Small-world (G2, G4), Random (G6), Log-normal degree distribution (G8), Quasi-scale-free (G10) network		

in Table 2.2, ensuring a variety of network characteristics for comparison. The total number of possible combinations of these simulation conditions is 25 × 6 = 150. The simulation period was set from 1 to 200, with each combination run 100 times.

3.2 New Product Diffusion Trajectories

In order to ascertain the impact of disparate simulation conditions on the diffusion pattern of a novel product, the temporal trajectories of diffusion are initially plotted and the discrepancies are elucidated. With a particular emphasis on the influence of setting pre-screening decisions prior to the final adoption decision, the simulations are classified into three distinct scenarios, contingent on the mean screening threshold and the designation of reference groups as either global or local. Each case is subsequently subdivided into subcases, thereby facilitating an investigation of the effects of other critical factors.

3.2.1 Overview of Simulated Diffusion Trajectories

Figure 3.1 depicts the complete set of trajectories generated by the simulation under all possible combinations of the conditions outlined in Table 3.1. Each trajectory is represented by a gray line, while the average diffusion curve for each network structure is represented by a distinct color. The figure illustrates that when simulations are conducted across a wide range of conditions, the diffusion trajectories display a notable degree of diversity, encompassing a spectrum from rapid ramp-up to minimal growth. However, it also demonstrates that under specific network structures, the diffusion trajectories diverge from those observed under alternative structures.

A comparison of the mean trajectories by network structure indicates that diffusion is the slowest in the regular network. This is an unsurprising outcome, given that each node possesses a limited constant number of links. As links are rewired, small-world networks emerge, and diffusion proceeds at a more rapid rate. If the links are further rewired, the small-world networks become purely random

Fig. 3.1 All trajectories of diffusion. Note: Colored lines represent the averages for a network: Black line for G0 (regular network); blue and green lines for G2, G4 (small-world network); magenta line for G6 (random network); yellow line for G8 (network with a log-normal degree distribution); red line for G10 (quasi scale-free network); grey lines for individual sample paths of simulation

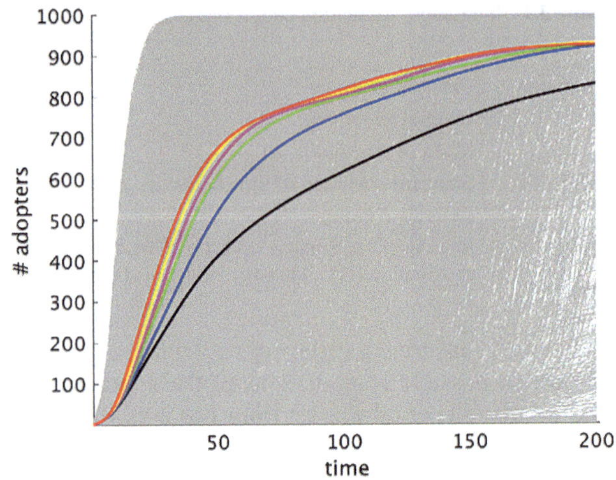

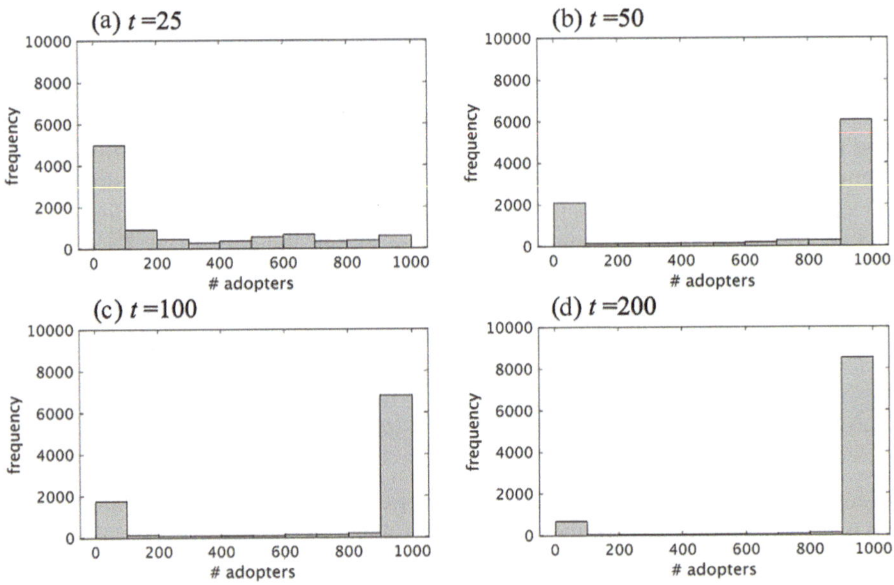

Fig. 3.2 Histograms of the number of adopters at $t = 25$, 50, 100, and 200 across simulations

networks. If rewiring follows the "preferential attachment" principle, the generated networks approach scale-free networks. The diffusion in these networks is even faster, and the differences between them are less pronounced.

A histogram of the number of adopters at each time point (Fig. 3.2) demonstrates that the distribution is not uniform. At $t = 25$, the majority of trajectories exhibit minimal or no diffusion. However, at $t = 50$, over half of the trajectories have been adopted by all agents, indicating a complete diffusion of 100%. Conversely, some trajectories continue to demonstrate minimal or no diffusion, with a limited number of occurrences of diffusion occurring. At time points $t = 100$ and $t = 200$, the number of trajectories that have achieved full diffusion increases, yet a few trajectories remain in which no diffusion occurs at all.

3.2.2 Scenario of Weak Screening

All potential combinations of simulation conditions are classified into three scenarios based on the parameters of pre-screening decision-making:

1) Weak screening: The mean of the screening threshold is equal to zero ($\mu = 0$). In this scenario, the pre-screening decision is essentially inconsequential.
2) Strong screening with global references: The mean of the threshold is high ($\mu = 0.10$). In this context, the reference group for each agent is the entire market.
3) Strong screening with local references: The mean of the threshold is high. Each agent's reference group is his/her neighbors on the network.

First of all, we consider the scenario of weak screening, which is divided into four subcases depending on the combination of levels of external/internal factors of adoption (π, θ). Figure 3.3 depicts the simulated diffusion trajectories for each subcase, where colored lines indicate the averages by network structure.

In the subcases with a strong external factor of adoption (Fig. 3.3a or b: $\pi = 0.01$), diffusion is rapid and exhibits minimal variation due to differences in network structure. Conversely, in the subcases with a weak external factor (Fig. 3.3c or d: $\pi = 0.001$), not only are diffusion trajectories more dispersed, but differences by network structure are also amplified. This can be explained by the fact that as the external factor of adoption weakens, the relative importance of influences from other agents increases, and thus their propagation efficiency becomes more dependent on the network structure. Furthermore, the comparison between Figs. 3.3 (a) and (c) suggest that the effect of the external factor of adoption is smaller than that of the internal factor.

3.2.3 Scenario of Strong Screening with Global References

We now turn to the scenario of strong screening with global references as defined above. A higher mean of the screening thresholds has the effect of suppressing early adoption, although the magnitude of this effect depends on the level of other factors. Figure 3.4 shows the diffusion trajectories in this case by subcase, corresponding to the combination of the external factor of adoption (π) and the standard deviation (inter-agent heterogeneity) of the screening threshold (σ). As can be seen clearly, there is considerable variation in both the pattern and the variability of diffusion trajectories across these subcases.

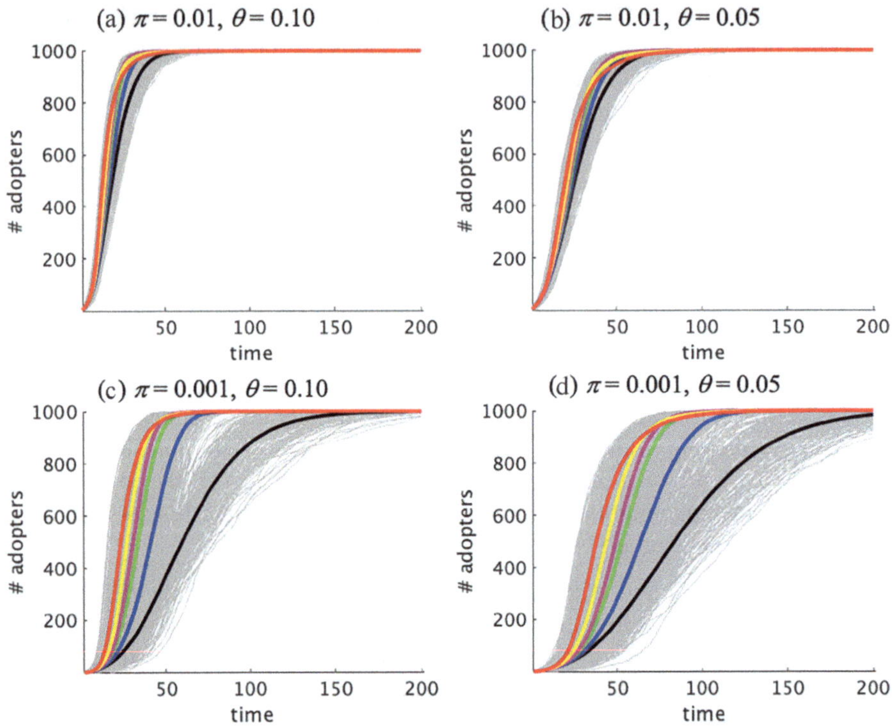

Fig. 3.3 Diffusion curves in the scenario of weak screening. Note: Colored lines represent the averages for a network: Black line for G0 (regular network); blue and green lines for G2, G4 (small-world network); magenta line for G6 (random network); yellow line for G8 (network with a log-normal degree distribution); red line for G10 (quasi scale-free network); grey lines for individual sample paths of simulation

In the scenario of strong screening with global references, we consider the baseline subcase in which the external factor of adoption is more pronounced ($\pi = 0.01$) and the inter-agent heterogeneity of the threshold is higher ($\sigma = 0.1$). The large σ creates a small number of agents (potential adopters) with a threshold of almost zero. These agents will pass the pre-screening stage even if the market-wide diffusion is negligible. Furthermore, since π is relatively large and the external factor is at work, these agents will ultimately adopt the new product. The average trajectories of diffusion appear not significantly different from the weak screening scenario, though the overall variation is magnified (Fig. 3.4a).

When the external factor of adoption is maintained at the baseline level ($\pi = 0.01$) and the standard deviation (heterogeneity) of the screening threshold is reduced from $\sigma = 0.1$ to 0.05, the overall variation of diffusion trajectories is significantly expanded to include seemingly stagnant trajectories, while the differences due to network structure remain relatively minor (Fig. 3.4b). Moreover, the onset of diffusion occurs later than in the baseline subcase, on average. In this subcase, the reduced heterogeneity makes it less likely that early adopters will emerge. However, once they do emerge, diffusion will proceed smoothly.

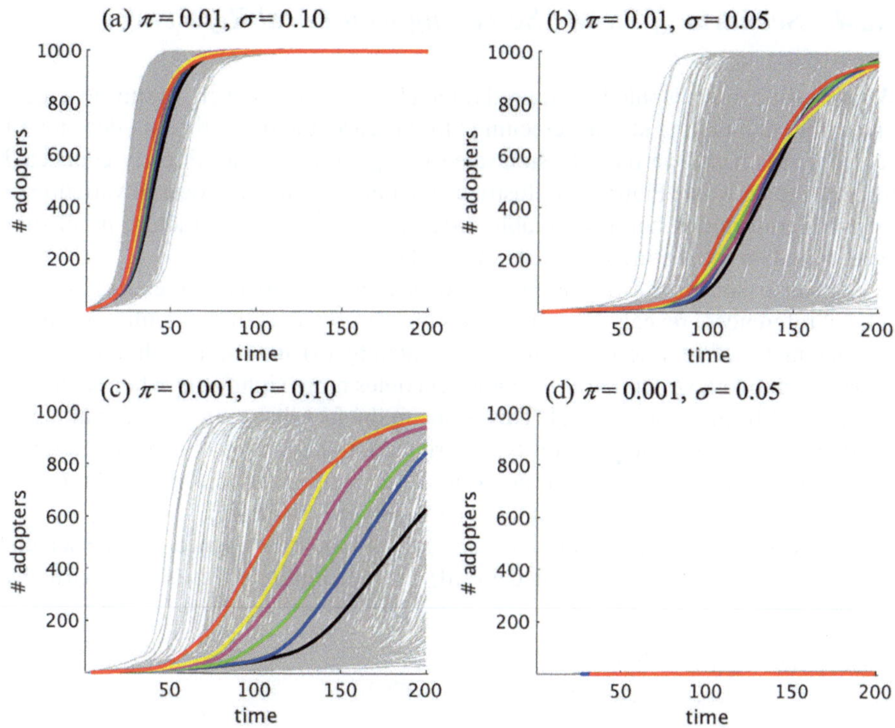

Fig. 3.4 Diffusion curves in the scenario of strong screening with global references. Note: Refer to the footnote of Fig. 3.3 for a definition of each colored line

Conversely, when the external factor of adoption is reduced from $\pi = 0.01$ to 0.001 and the heterogeneity of the threshold remains at the baseline level ($\sigma = 0.1$), both the overall variation in diffusion trajectories and the differences due to network structure are amplified (Fig. 3.4c). When the external factor of adoption is reduced, the effect of the internal factor, such as word-of-mouth (WOM) communication, becomes more pronounced. In this subcase, a greater number of agents with a sufficiently low threshold can successfully navigate the pre-screening process and adopt a new product due to the influence of the internal factor. The heightened interdependence among agents on the basis of their network connections gives rise to notable variations in diffusion trajectories across different network structures.

Ultimately, when both the external factor of adoption and the heterogeneity of the threshold are smaller ($\pi = 0.001$, $\sigma = 0.05$) than the baseline subcase, minimal diffusion occurs even at $t = 200$ (Fig. 3.4d). In other words, for diffusion to occur in strong screening with global references, at least one of the following conditions must be met: firstly, there must be high heterogeneity in the screening threshold, whereby a certain number of agents pass pre-screening even at a stage when the overall market diffusion is small. Secondly, there must be subcases with a strong external factor of adoption, whereby even if a small number of agents can pass at the pre-screening stage, they are more likely to subsequently adopt it regardless of the market diffusion environment.

3.2.4 Scenario of Strong Screening with Local References

What modifications would be required if the global reference were to shift to a local one while maintaining strong screening? In this case, the pre-screening decision of each agent is based on the diffusion rate of neighbors who are directly connected through the network. Figure 3.5 illustrates not only a significant overall variation in diffusion trajectories but also notable differences by network structure in all sub-cases based on the distinctive values of π and σ.

A comparison of the results presented in Figs. 3.5 (local references) and 3.4 (global references) reveals several noteworthy observations. In particular, when the external factor of adoption is strong (represented by (a) and (b) in both figures), the impact of network structure on outcomes becomes more significant when reference groups shift from global to local. This is due to the fact that a strong external factor of adoption increases the probability of early adoption. Conversely, when reference groups are local, the influence of the external factor of adoption is more contingent, and subsequent diffusion is dependent on the network structure.

Secondly, when the external factor is weak and the heterogeneity of the screening threshold is small (represented by (d) in both figures), diffusion is virtually

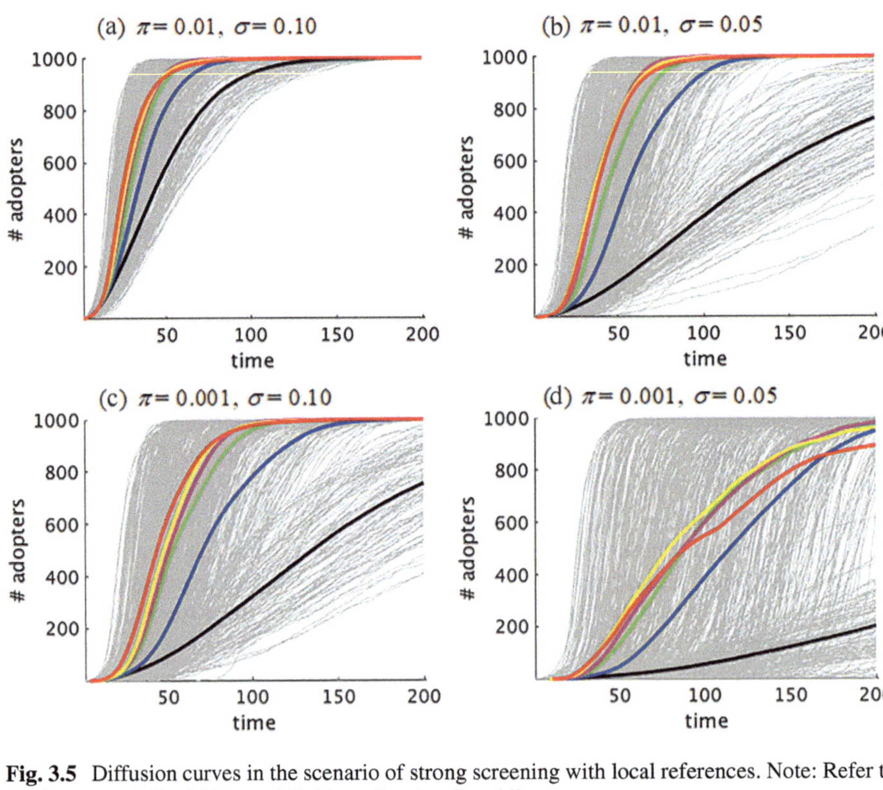

Fig. 3.5 Diffusion curves in the scenario of strong screening with local references. Note: Refer to the footnote of Fig. 3.3 for a definition of each colored line

non-existent when reference groups are global. However, when they are local, diffusion does occur, albeit with considerable differences. This is also due to the fact that, when reference groups are local, the probability of adoption occurring by chance within one's own reference group is more uncertain.

This study aims to explore the influence of network structure on the speed and pattern of diffusion. In all subcases, diffusion within the regular network is significantly slower, as it is less likely that local diffusion surpasses the threshold in a network lacking nodes with a certain degree or higher. The second slowest diffusion, on average, occurs in the small-world network, which closely resembles the regular network. In these networks, clustering coefficients are higher, and the spread of information or influence is less efficient. The difference among other networks, including quasi-scale-free networks, may be minimal. Notably, networks with a few hubs of very high degree do not dominate. Further rigorous analyses will be presented in the next subsection.

3.3 Impacts on the Net Present Value of Diffusion

The diffusion rates presented in the preceding section exhibit temporal fluctuations. Marketers must consider not only the eventual level of diffusion but also the timeline for achieving that level. Net Present Value (NPV) serves as a comprehensive metric for assessing these aspects (see Eq. 2.5 in Sect. 2.2.2 for the definition). We analyze the relationship between NPV and simulation conditions using regression analyses. All predictor variables are binary, taking values of 0 or 1. For network structure, the baseline is set to G4, and the estimated coefficient for each network structure indicates its relative contribution to the NPV. For other predictors, the baseline is Level 1 (Table 3.1).

3.3.1 Estimation of Regression Models with Main Effects

The profit in each period is aggregated into the NPV using a fixed discount rate. The selection of the discount rate reflects marketers' time preferences: if they prioritize profits in the distant future, the discount rate should be set low; if they prioritize profits closer to the present, the discount rate should be set high. Here, the NPV is computed at three discount rates $d = 5\%$, 10%, and 20%, while previous studies on diffusion have typically assumed $d = 10\%$ and a time unit of years.

To quantify how network structures and other conditions influence diffusion, we regress $\ln(1 + \text{NPV})$ on dummy variables for the simulation conditions. Initially, interaction effects are disregarded, and a model with main effects only is estimated. The estimation results are presented in Table 3.2 and can be summarized as follows:

1. Compared to the case with G4 (baseline), the cases with G0 (regular network) and G2 (small-world network near regular network) have significantly lower

Table 3.2 Regression analysis on NPV with the main effects on the NPV

	NPV (d = 5%)			NPV (d = 10%)			NPV (d = 20%)		
	Estimate	s.e.		Estimate	s.e.		Estimate	s.e.	
Const.	4.587	.031	s	3.361	.026	s	2.175	.021	s
G0	−.483	.033	s	−.350	.027	s	−.157	.022	s
G2	−.189	.033	s	−.174	.027	s	−.094	.022	s
G6	.073	.033	b	.077	.027	a	.036	.022	
G8	.149	.033	s	.173	.027	s	.115	.022	s
G10	.218	.033	s	.277	.027	s	.224	.022	s
π	1.555	.019	s	1.827	.016	s	1.876	.013	s
θ	.469	.019	s	.562	.016	s	.449	.013	s
μ	−2.167	.019	s	−2.285	.016	s	−2.026	.013	s
σ	.906	.019	s	.794	.016	s	.597	.013	s
Ref	−.952	.019	s	−.733	.016	s	−.436	.013	s
N	9600			9600			9600		
R^2	.731			.811			.840		

Note: s: $p < .001$; a: $p < .01$; b: $p < .05$; c: $p < .10$; the baseline for network dummy variables is set to G4. The reference group dummy (*ref*) takes 1 if the reference group is global. The other dummies correspond to the level with the highest value in each condition

NPV regardless of the discount rate (d); in contrast, it is significantly higher in the cases G8 and G10 (networks with fewer hubs). The difference between the cases G4 and G6 (purely random network) is small and no longer significant when $d = 20\%$ (the profits in the future are less emphasized).

2. If the external or internal factor of adoption (π, θ) is larger, the NPV increases significantly.
3. When the mean of the screening threshold (μ) is large (indicating strong screening) or reference groups for it (ref) are global, the NPV decreases; in contrast, when the standard deviation of the threshold (σ) is large, the NPV increases.
4. Notably, the coefficient of determination (R^2) of the model slightly increases as the discount rate rises, suggesting that other omitted factors influencing adoption could have less impact when more emphasis is placed on present profit.

Among the above findings, the first one (the effects of network structure on NPV) indicates that networks with a few hubs, typically scale-free networks, are superior communication channels among potential adopters, even in terms of NPV. Other simulation conditions also have significant effects. It is straightforward to understand why the external and internal factors of adoption (π, θ) have a positive effect on NPV. Rather, an explanation is needed for the expected signs of the mean (μ) and standard deviation (σ) of the screening threshold. As discussed in Sect. 3.2.3, the larger the mean (μ), the fewer potential adopters who can pass the pre-screening stage (hence its coefficient is negative). On the other hand, the larger the standard deviation (σ), the greater the number of potential adopters with a lower screening threshold.

3.3.2 *Estimation of Regression Models with Added Interaction Effects*

Visual inspection in Sect. 3.1 clearly suggests that there will be a wide range of interactions among the simulation conditions. We must therefore estimate a regression model that accounts for multiple interactions of simulation conditions to measure their effect on the NPV. The dummy variables μ and ref. are replaced by the following two dummy variables: one corresponding to the case where strong screening (μ = 0.1) is performed under the global reference group, and the other corresponding to the case where it is performed based on the local reference group. Both dummy variables take the value zero in the case of weak screening. After further variable selection, the final model assumes that the external factor of adoption (π) interacts with network structure (***G***), the internal factor of adoption (θ), and the heterogeneity in the screening threshold (σ), all of which interact with differences in pre-screening behavior.

The dependent variable, NPV, depends on the discount rate. Therefore, we will perform a regression analysis on NPV under a discount rate of 10%, a commonly used rate in many studies. The three columns on the left of Table 3.3 show the results for the weak screening case. The middle three columns represent the differential effects of moving from weak screening to strong screening with a global reference, and the right three columns represent the differential effects of moving from

Table 3.3 Regression analysis on NPV with interaction terms: d = 10%

		When weak			Shift to strong screening					
		Screening			w/ Global Ref.			w/ Local Ref.		
		Estimate	s.e.		Estimate	s.e.		Estimate	s.e.	
Const.		3.363	.027	s	−2.749	.047	s	−3.334	.047	s
	G0	−.575	.033	s	−.105	.057	c	.553	.057	s
	G2	−.286	.033	s	−.110	.057	c	.316	.057	s
	G6	.107	.033	a	−.034	.057		−.062	.057	
	G8	.342	.033	s	−.139	.057		−.355	.057	s
	G10	.625	.033	s	−.358	.057	s	−.540	.057	s
π		1.861	.038	s	.617	.066	s	−.675	.066	s
π	×G0	.425	.047	s	−.330	.081	s	−.467	.081	s
π	×G2	.214	.047	s	−.089	.081		−.286	.081	a
π	×G6	−.071	.047		.226	.081	a	.008	.081	
π	×G8	−.262	.047	s	.309	.081	s	.368	.081	s
π	×G10	−.492	.047	s	.465	.081	s	.512	.081	s
θ		.875	.019	s	.166	.033	s	−.547	.033	s
σ		−.129	.019	s	1.790	.033	s	1.106	.033	s
$\pi \times \theta$		−.465	.027	s	−.028	.047		.146	.047	s
$\pi \times \sigma$		.063	.027		−.419	.047	s	1.762	.047	s
					N =	9600		R^2 =	.929	

Note: s: $p < .001$; a: $p < .01$; b: $p < .05$; c: $p < .10$

weak screening to strong screening with a local reference. Let us compare the statistically significant results with those of the main-effect-only model, starting with the weak screening case:

1. Despite the inclusion of interaction terms, the sole effect of each variable is almost consistent in significance and sign to the results of the main-effects-only model (Table 3.2). That is, NPV increases as the network structure changes from a regular network (G0) to a network with a small number of hubs (G10), and as the external and internal factors of adoption (π, θ) strengthen.
2. The effect of heterogeneity in the screening threshold (σ) was positive in the main-effects-only model but negative in the weak screening case. This inconsistency suggests a non-negligible interaction between threshold heterogeneity and screening strength or reference group. In the case of weak screening (where the mean of thresholds is zero), the increased variation in thresholds across agents results in many agents who do not consider adopting the new product at the screening stage.
3. The interaction between the external factor of adoption (π) and network structure is positive for G0 and G2 and negative for G8 and G10, which means that the increased external factor suppresses the effect of network structure (i.e., the difference between networks becomes smaller).
4. The interaction effect between the external and internal factors of adoption (π, θ) is negative, suggesting that they can cancel each other out. This negative synergy between π and θ may be derived from the formulation of the individual-level adoption model

Next, we will look at the differential effect when moving to strong screening (i.e., note that it is not the overall effect of the case of strong screening)

5. The coefficient of the dummy variable for switching to high screening is negative, with a more pronounced effect when reference groups are global. Consequently, the NPV is lower in the case of strong screening compared to weak screening, and even lower when reference groups are global. This result is not unexpected, as screening generally delays the adoption process.
6. The interaction effect with network structure is positive for G0 and G2 but negative for G8 and G10, indicating that the differential effect of network structure is reduced. However, when interactions with the external factor are introduced, the opposite effect reemerges, particularly when reference groups are global. To capture the overall effect, we will later calculate the predicted values of the dummy variable combinations.
7. The positive effect of the external or internal factors of adoption (π, θ) in the case of weak screening is diminished in the strong screening scenario with global references, while it is amplified in the case with local references. Screening with global references suppresses adoption even when the external and internal factors of adoption are strong, resulting in their reduced effects. The opposite holds true in a scenario with local references, particularly as the effects of the external factor are more likely to drive adoption.

8. The negative effect of heterogeneity in screening thresholds (σ) in the case of weak screening is reversed in the case of strong screening, whether with global or local references. Even when the mean threshold is high, greater interpersonal differences allow a small number of potential adopters with thresholds close to zero to pass the screening decision stage and proceed to the adoption decision stage.

There are more intricate interactions among the simulation conditions. In the case of strong screening with global references, the negative interaction between π and θ observed in the weak screening scenario diminishes. Furthermore, a positive interaction between π and σ, which was not observed in the weak screening scenario, emerges. With local references, a negative interaction between π and σ arises. The interpretation of these interactions can lead to complex discussions; therefore, we will refrain from further analysis in this matter.

What would be the impact of adjusting the discount rate to $d = 5\%$ or 20% on the aforementioned outcomes? Table 3.3 ($d = 10\%$), Table 3.4 ($d = 5\%$), and Table 3.5 ($d = 20\%$) can be compared to identify the variables that exhibit differences in terms of their significance and direction. In the weak screening scenario, the direction of the significant effects of the various conditions is largely independent of the discount rate, indicating that the discount rate does not qualitatively impact the results.

In the scenario of strong screening with a global reference, only the effect of external factors (π) changes direction with the discount rate: positive for $d = 5\%$, but negative for $d = 10\%$ or $d = 20\%$. Even under this scenario, a stronger external factor

Table 3.4 Regression analysis on NPV with interaction terms: $d = 5\%$

		When weak			Shift to strong screening					
		Screening			w/ Global Ref.			w/ Local Ref.		
		Estimate	s.e.		Estimate	s.e.		Estimate	s.e.	
Const.		4.773	.027	s	−2.523	−96.775	s	−4.677	−53.707	s
	G0	−.670	.034	s	−.642	9.725	s	.566	−11.042	s
	G2	−.273	.034	s	−.263	4.567	s	.266	−4.519	s
	G6	.097	.034	s	−.018	.197		.011	−.301	
	G8	.257	.034	s	−.041	−2.516		−.146	−.702	b
	G10	.427	.034	s	−.293	−1.714	s	−.100	−5.045	c
π		1.160	.039	s	1.206	9.677	s	.812	15.540	s
π	×G0	.549	.047	s	−.019	−6.419		−.528	−.230	s
π	×G2	.218	.047	s	.055	−3.235		−.266	.674	a
π	×G6	−.072	.047		.157	−.680	c	−.056	1.906	
π	×G8	−.208	.047	s	.178	2.021		.166	2.167	b
π	×G10	−.353	.047	s	.405	1.528	s	.126	4.925	
θ		.664	.019	s	.329	−12.969	s	−.242	4.025	s
σ		−.101	.019	s	1.864	56.424	s	1.863	56.463	s
$\pi \times \theta$		−.388	.027	s	−.220	8.963	s	.038	3.526	
$\pi \times \sigma$		.063	.027		−.971	26.487	s	1.321	−21.779	s
					$N =$	9600		$R^2 =$	.928	

Note: s: $p < .001$; a: $p < .01$; b: $p < .05$; c: $p < .10$

Table 3.5 Regression analysis on NPV with interaction terms: $d = 20\%$

		When weak			Shift to strong screening					
		Screening			w/ Global Ref.			w/ Local Ref.		
		Estimate	s.e.		Estimate	s.e.		Estimate	s.e.	
Const.		1.992	.026	s	−1.891	.045	s	−1.986	.044	s
	G0	−.263	.032	s	.046	.055		.260	.055	s
	G2	−.159	.032	s	.009	.055		.184	.055	a
	G6	.032	.032		−.056	.055		.002	.055	
	G8	.237	.032	s	−.212	.055	s	−.256	.055	s
	G10	.532	.032	s	−.389	.055	s	−.505	.055	s
π		2.309	.036	s	−.843	.063	s	−1.514	.063	s
π	$\times G0$	.133	.045	a	−.128	.077		−.169	.077	b
π	$\times G2$	.094	.045	b	−.092	.077		−.146	.077	c
π	$\times G6$	.002	.045		.197	.077	b	−.063	.077	
π	$\times G8$	−.145	.045	a	.303	.077	s	.240	.077	a
π	$\times G10$	−.359	.045	s	.356	.077	s	.408	.077	s
θ		.713	.018	s	−.215	.032	s	−.542	.032	s
σ		−.080	.018	s	1.051	.032	s	.698	.032	s
$\pi \times \theta$		−.241	.026	s	.287	.045	s	.076	.045	b
$\pi \times \sigma$		−.015	.026		.649	.045	s	1.332	.045	s
					$N =$	9600		$R^2 =$	.920	

Note: s: $p < .001$; a: $p < .01$; b: $p < .05$; c: $p < .10$

promotes adoption but with a delay. When $d = 5\%$, the NPV remains unchanged regardless of the delay, as long as the same level of diffusion is eventually achieved. Thus, the effect of the external factor is positive. However, when $d = 10\%$ or 20%, the delay in diffusion reduces the NPV. Consequently, the external factor is less effective than in the weak screening scenario.

In the scenario of strong screening with local references, the delay in diffusion is less significant than in the scenario with global references. However, there is a broader range of variables for which the direction of the effect changes with the discount rate. It is important to emphasize that the impact of the internal factor becomes negative only when $d = 20\%$. Consequently, the positive effect observed in the weak screening scenario is nullified in this scenario. This outcome can be interpreted as a delay in diffusion, which manifests as a reduction in the word-of-mouth (WOM) effect within the neighborhood when the discount rate is high and greater emphasis is placed on early adoption following the introduction of a new product in the NPV calculation.

3.3.3 Visualizing the Overall Effects of Simulation Conditions

In order to gain intuitive insight into the impact of each simulation condition on the net present value (NPV), it is beneficial to present a graphical representation of the NPV predicted by the regression model described in the previous subsection for each combination of conditions. Figure 3.6 illustrates the predicted NPV with the moderate discount rate ($d = 10\%$), demonstrating that differences in screening scenarios exert a greater impact on the NPV than other factors. In the scenario of weak screening, the impacts of external and internal adoption factors (π, θ) are more pronounced than those observed in network structure. The NPV is largest when both factors are relatively strong ($\pi = 0.01$, $\theta = 0.10$).

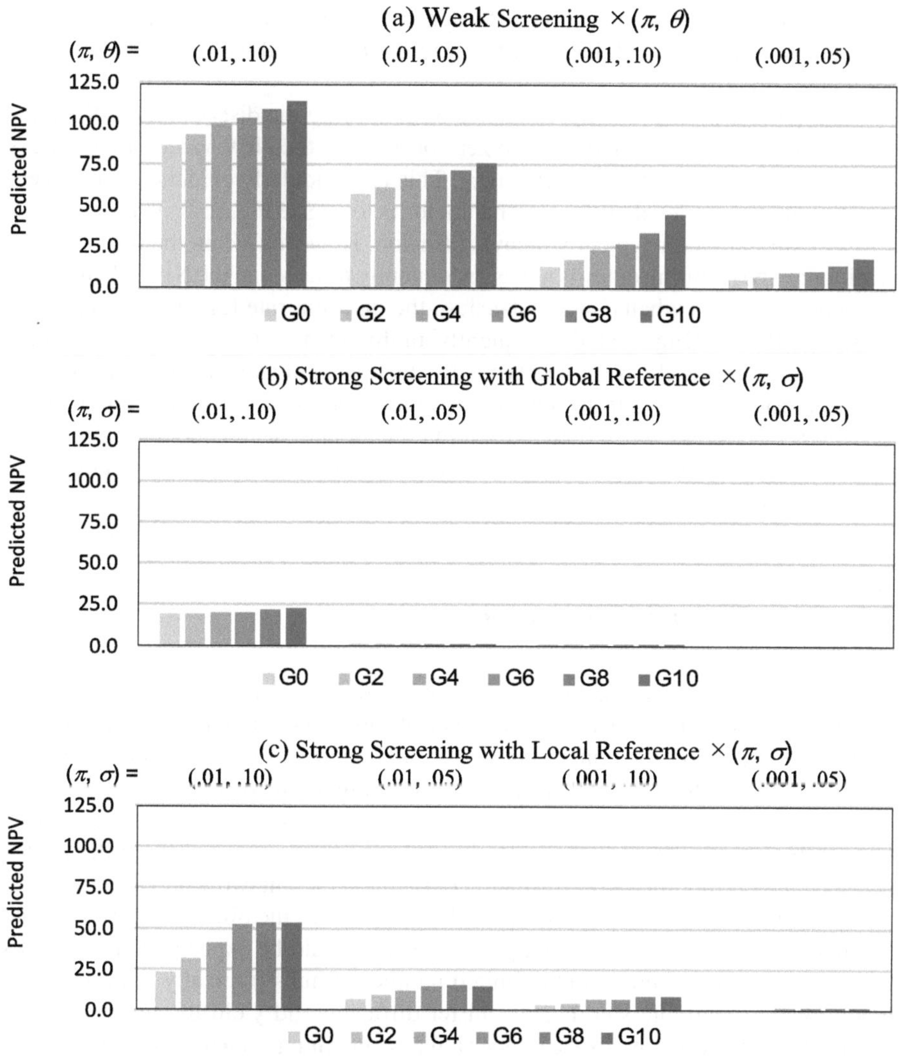

Fig. 3.6 Predicted values of NPV given simulation conditions when $d = 10\%$. Note: The weak screening scenarios are divided into four subcases by the levels of π (external factor of adoption) and of θ (internal factor of adoption); The strong screening scenarios are divided into four subcases by the levels of π and by the levels of σ (heterogeneity of screening threshold). In addition, G0, G2, G4, G6, G8, and G10 represent different network structures (see Table 3.1)

The NPV is markedly smaller in the scenario of strong screening than in the scenario of weak screening. As in Sect. 3.2, four subcases are created under the strong screening scenario, combining high or low external factors with high or low threshold heterogeneity. In particular, the NPV is nearly zero for subcases in strong screening with global references, with the exception of the subcase where both levels of the external factor of adoption and the threshold heterogeneity are relatively high ($\pi = 0.01$, $\sigma = 0.10$), where slight diffusion occurs (see Fig. 3.4d). In the case of local references, the NPV is non-zero but markedly smaller than in the weak screening scenario. The impact on NPV appears to be influenced by network structure exclusively when both levels of the external factor and the threshold heterogeneity are high.

Finally, we will examine the influence of modifying the discount rate. When the discount rate is set to a value close to zero or $d = 5\%$, the NPV values are typically higher than those obtained with $d = 10\%$. This is particularly evident when screening is weak and the level of the external factor is low (See Fig. 3.7). This is because a weak external factor typically delays diffusion. However, when the discount rate is minimal, the resulting delay is not as prominently reflected in the NPV. Conversely, the opposite occurs when $d = 20\%$ because the discount rate functions as a penalty for slow diffusion (Fig. 3.8). Consequently, in the strong screening scenario, where diffusion is delayed, the NPV will typically decline significantly. In a weak screening scenario, the NPV still decreases when the external factor of adoption is weak ($\pi = 0.001$). However, when both the external factor and the threshold heterogeneity are both large ($\pi = 0.01$, $\sigma = 0.10$), the NPV does not decrease because almost no delay occurs.

3.4 Summary and Discussion

Three scenarios were simulated using the extended GLM model: weak screening, strong screening with global references, and strong screening with local references. In the first scenario, potential adopters (agents) conduct little to no pre-screening and make adoption decisions similarly to the original GLM model. In the second scenario, each agent makes a pre-screening decision based on whether the market-wide diffusion rate exceeds their threshold. In the third scenario, the criterion for pre-screening is modified to the diffusion rate among their network-linked neighbors.

The simulation results provide valuable insights into the diffusion phenomenon. From a network structure-oriented perspective, it would be expected that networks where links are concentrated in a limited number of hubs (typically scale-free networks) would facilitate significantly faster diffusion and yield the highest NPVs. While this expectation holds true under a weak screening scenario, it does not necessarily apply under a strong screening scenario. This outcome is influenced by behavioral parameters, such as external and internal factors of adoption, the heterogeneity of thresholds, and other conditions. Additionally, the discount rate plays a crucial role in evaluating the NPV to reflect marketers' time preferences.

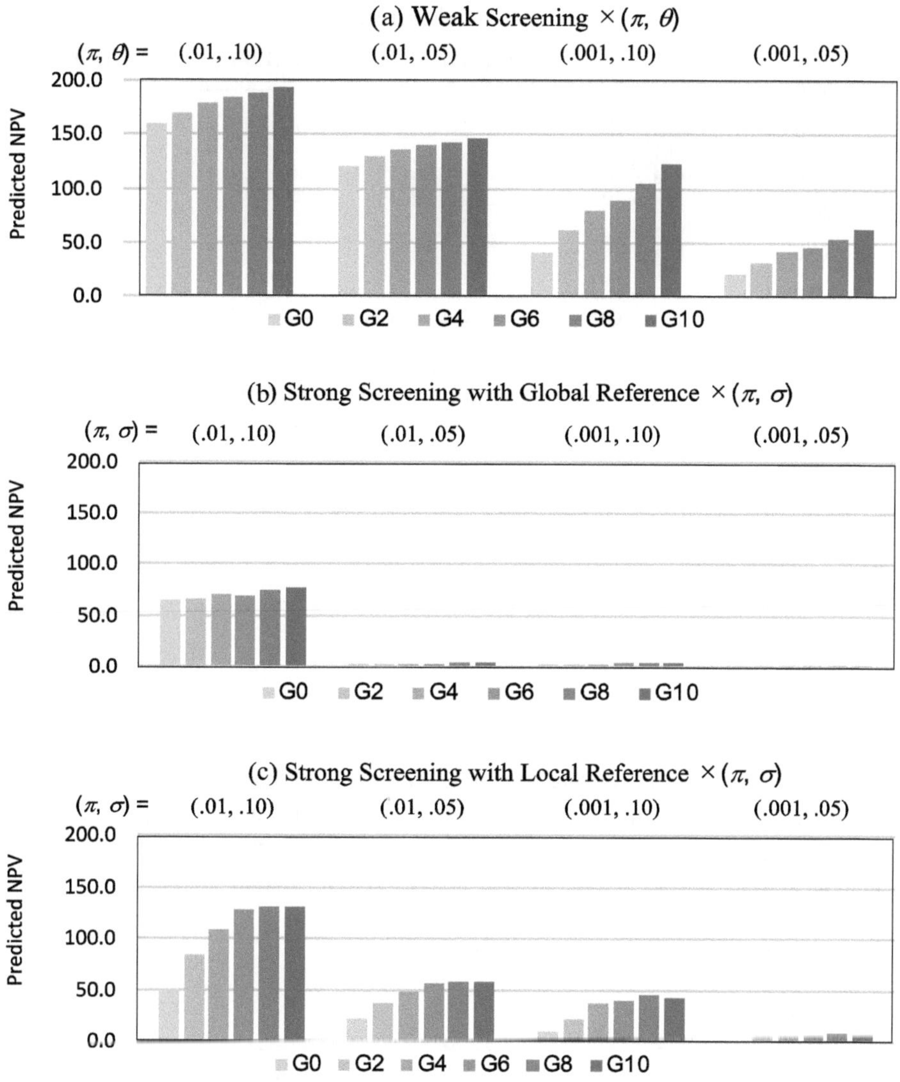

Fig. 3.7 Expected values of NPV given simulation conditions when $d = 5\%$. Note: Refer to the footnote in Table 3.6 for details

In scenarios involving strong screening, there are cases where diffusion occurs minimally or not at all. There are also cases where diffusion occurs on average, including those under weak screening scenarios, but with substantial stochastic variation. It is fair to say that both cases constitute diffusion failure. Whether diffusion is likely to fail is predicted more accurately by differences in behavioral parameters than by differences in network structure. This should be considered by marketers attempting to introduce new products. Traditional diffusion models have

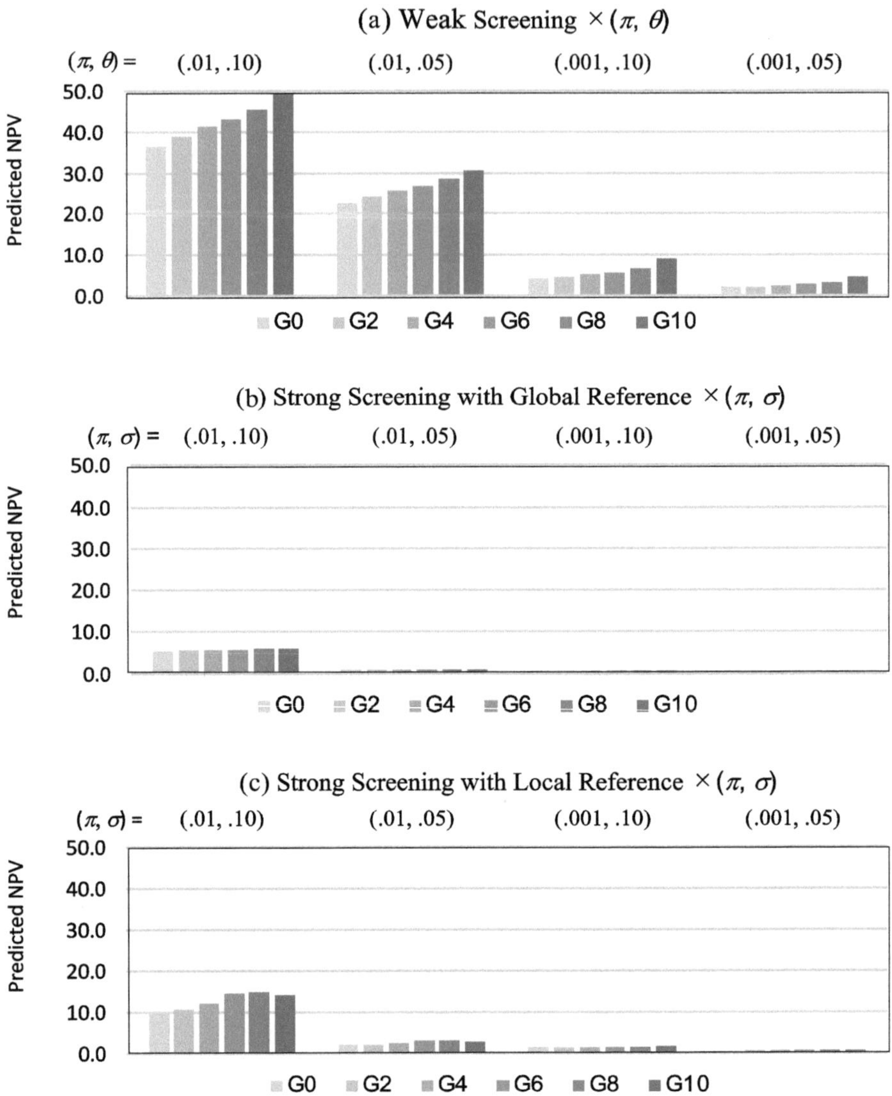

Fig. 3.8 Expected values of NPV given simulation conditions when $d = 20\%$. Note: Refer to the footnote in Table 3.6 for details

not provided a clear answer to diffusion failure, which is a major concern for marketers. For instance, the Bass model can address this by predetermining a low upper limit for diffusion, which appears somewhat tautological. In this regard, the model presented in this chapter offers notable progress.

Another possible formulation is that the adoption decision is based solely on threshold-based screening. Granovetter [71] proposed a model in which decisions are made based on whether the diffusion rate exceeds a certain threshold, resulting in a single-stage decision-making process. Similarly, Watts and Dodds [166] applied the threshold model to information propagation—a form of diffusion phenomenon—on a network. They developed a model in which the probability of a decision increases with the frequency of exposure to information and compared it to the behavior of the threshold model. This can be considered an adaptation of the GLM model with only the internal factor. It is important to note that when the threshold model alone is assumed, considering the network structure among agents is meaningful only when reference groups are local.

It is possible to consider, for example, the bandwagon effect [97] operating alongside network externalities as a basis for threshold-based pre-screening decisions. The effect of network externalities arises from the economic benefits gained due to the high number of product adopters and does not necessarily involve communication. In contrast, the bandwagon effect can stem from psychological conformity, where individuals follow the behavior of the majority or their peer group. The simplest mechanism behind this effect is likely peer pressure. Additionally, it can be interpreted as bounded rational behavior, wherein potential adopters, faced with uncertainty regarding the quality of a new product, form their preferences based on the adoption decisions of others. This aligns with the theory that agents make adaptive decisions to minimize cognitive costs, as discussed in Sect. 2.4.

Chapter 4
Application for Influencer Marketing

In recent years, the concept of influencer marketing has emerged as a prominent area of focus within the field of marketing research [30, 73, 99]. Influencers are a relatively small number of individuals who exert significant influence over others. In influencer marketing, the process of identifying these influencers and employing them as seeds to spread word-of-mouth (or nonverbal influence) broadly to other potential customers is referred to as seeding. This chapter provides an overview of prior research on seeding, followed by a simulation analysis of seeding effects in a hypothetical network using the agent-based diffusion model constructed in Chap. 3. Additionally, it discusses desirable seeding strategies through simulations using social media data observed in the real world.

4.1 Review of Influencer Research

Although the term "influencer" has gained prominence in recent years, similar concepts have existed for a long time. One of the most notable of these is the concept of "opinion leaders," which originated in social psychology and was later adopted in marketing research. With the rise of network science, the role of "hubs," or nodes with a significantly higher number of links in social networks, has attracted considerable attention. Researchers have conducted both empirical and theoretical studies to assess the effectiveness of targeting these hubs in marketing campaigns. Meanwhile, network science has developed more sophisticated influencer metrics, surpassing simple measures such as degree centrality (i.e., the number of links in a network). Before delving into our research, it is valuable to trace the evolution of these interconnected studies.

M. Mizuno, *Complex Modeling of Consumer Behavior*, Evolutionary Economics and Social Complexity Science 34,
https://doi.org/10.1007/978-4-431-54874-4_4

4.1.1 Prehistory of Influencer Research

A significant advancement in opinion leader research is the measurement and analysis of the social networks of potential adopters [37, 85]. These studies are closely related to the field of social network analysis within sociology. Later, the study of complex networks emerged in the disciplines of physics and mathematics, leading to the development of the interdisciplinary field of network science [107, 124].

Network science utilizes various measures of network centrality to quantify the importance of nodes within a network. The most fundamental of these is degree centrality, which refers to the number of nodes connected to a given node. This can be likened to the number of followers on Twitter. Nodes with significantly higher degree centrality than others are termed hubs, and their importance has been acknowledged across various disciplines [11]. The strategy of selecting hubs as seeds (hereafter referred to as hub seeding) has been widely advocated in books for general audiences and has gained considerable popularity among marketers [60, 143].

4.1.2 Empirical Studies on Hub Seeding

Several studies have employed empirical methods to investigate the effects of hub seeding, yielding at least partially positive results. Some studies assess the effectiveness of seeding in terms of behavioral changes among targets, such as word-of-mouth diffusion and purchases, while others evaluate its impact on customer lifetime value [93, 102].

One methodological approach in these empirical studies involves field experiments, conducted primarily offline [45, 61, 77], online [69], or both [160]. All of these approaches incorporate experimental designs in which seeding is exogenously controlled, taking into account the degree centrality of each individual in the customer network. Another category of research involves quantitative analysis of data gathered from online environments. Performance metrics include examining individual users' media consumption, posting activity, and purchasing behavior [62, 68, 161]. Furthermore, simulation studies utilize actual observed social networks [102, 108].

Conversely, several empirical studies focusing on social media seeding have reported negative findings regarding the effects of hub seeding [10, 84, 89, 96, 144]. It is evident that drawing generalized conclusions about the efficacy of seeding strategies based on empirical evidence presents a considerable challenge. This complexity arises from the fact that the effectiveness of a given strategy is contingent upon a variety of factors, including the evaluation indicators used, the individuals targeted (seeds), the properties of the networks connecting them, the content of the word-of-mouth messages propagated, and the characteristics of the surrounding environment.

4.1.3 Critique from an ROI Perspective

In general, hub seeding is considered the most effective method for propagating word-of-mouth within a network. However, the findings of Watts and Dodds [166] in a simulation study challenge this notion and warrant further consideration. The efficacy of seeding was assessed through the simulation of word-of-mouth diffusion within a virtual network. The performance metric employed was the size of the cascade generated by seeding—roughly equivalent to the diffusion rate—divided by the number of nodes directly influenced by the seed, also referred to as degree centrality. The researchers concluded that hub seeding is only superior to random seeding under fairly specific and limited conditions. According to this evaluation criterion, if the seed is a hub, its degree is, by definition, larger, meaning that the performance of hub seeding will be lower unless the incremental word-of-mouth penetration surpasses the incremental degree of the seed.

Bakshy et al. [9] further expanded the Watts-Dodds framework by introducing a scenario in which the cost of seeding per seed increases with the seed's degree. If the marketer has control over the level of investment, relying solely on ROI as an objective may not be appropriate. This is because, if the return function is concave, ROI can be maximized by minimizing the investment level. In such a case, it may be more prudent to define the objective function not solely by ROI, but by the overall profit, subtracting costs from revenues. The evaluation of hub seeding could therefore vary depending on the chosen evaluation criterion.

4.1.4 Studies on Optimal Seeding Algorithm

Although degree centrality is a relatively straightforward method for seeding, it has the drawback of not fully capturing the intricate properties of the network. In their textbooks, scholars of network science introduce various centrality indices beyond degree centrality, including closeness centrality, betweenness centrality, and PageRank, among others [124]. As the network size increases, the exact calculation of these measures becomes increasingly challenging, necessitating some form of approximation. When applying these techniques to real-world influencer marketing, it is crucial to ensure that the computational burden remains manageable.

More advanced seeding algorithms have been proposed in the field of computer science for scenarios where information or influence is propagated, extending beyond traditional centrality measures (e.g., [33, 88, 98, 155]). These algorithms require a comprehensive and detailed understanding of the network, which, in turn, imposes a substantial computational burden. To address this challenge, some studies have sought to refine the previously employed centrality measures [130, 168]. Alternatively, research has focused on algorithms for more effective seeding that rely solely on local information about the network [14, 51, 80, 81, 109].

In practice, additional information beyond network properties may be available among potential adopters and could be leveraged for seeding purposes. For instance, Haenlein and Libai [74] propose targeting customers with high customer lifetime value as revenue leaders, regardless of network-related information. This approach can be implemented using historical purchase data alone. Furthermore, algorithms have been proposed that integrate both network characteristics and individual attributes measured outside the network, offering a more holistic approach to seeding [34, 57].

4.1.5 Further Considerations for Effective Seeding

In the context of seeding data from social media, analyzing the content of users' posts can provide valuable insights for targeting purposes. Lambrecht et al. [95] proposed seeding users who had posted words that appeared in Twitter trends at an early stage, designating them as "early trend propagators." Furthermore, it is expected that the influence and susceptibility of each user can be assessed through social media communications, which can then be leveraged in seeding strategies [3, 4, 15]. Even when hubs are targeted for seeding, the overall effectiveness of the strategy may diminish if their influence and the susceptibility of their followers are significantly weaker. An algorithm that calibrates the influence of influencers and the susceptibility of their followers using actual social media data to determine the optimal seeding strategy has been proposed by Mizuno et al. [112]. A brief discussion of this study is provided in Sect. 4.3.

In social media post analysis, sentiment analysis is a widely used method for quantifying content valence, categorizing it as positive, negative, or neutral (e.g., [91, 92]). The strategies that marketers adopt depend on whether the word-of-mouth surrounding their company and its products is positive or negative. In the case of a new product, if early adopters are dissatisfied and share negative feedback, non-adopters who come across such feedback are likely to lower their adoption intentions. Goldenberg et al. [63] further explore this phenomenon by extending the GLM model to incorporate mechanisms for negative word-of-mouth in an agent-based diffusion model.

Recent research has shifted its focus from merely identifying highly influential seeds to understanding how these seeds can be influenced in ways beneficial to marketers. In practice, individuals identified as influencers often seek to monetize their influence and expect compensation from firms. It is therefore crucial to recognize that seeding typically incurs costs, particularly in terms of influencer remuneration. The challenge of designing effective incentives to motivate influencers has emerged as a key topic in influencer research [58, 82, 129]. It should be noted that if motivating effective influencers proves challenging, an alternative strategy may involve seeding average individuals [154].

4.2 Evaluating Seeding Strategies on Complex Networks

In this section, we assess the effectiveness of the hub seeding strategy by extending the agent-based new product diffusion model introduced in Chap. 3. The seeding strategy is integrated into the model by specifying a seeding rate of $r \times 100\%$ of all potential adopters as having already adopted the new product at the initial time point $t = 0$. From $t = 1$ onward, the same mechanism described in Chap. 3 is applied. The overall performance of hub seeding is evaluated based on profit, defined as the resulting net present value (NPV) minus the total seeding costs. This performance measure is then compared with those of random seeding and no seeding. The optimal seeding strategy and rate can be determined based on specific cost conditions, adoption behavior settings, and network structure.

4.2.1 *Simulation and Evaluation Procedure*

Three distinct seeding strategies are considered: hub seeding ($s = 1$), which selects seeds based on the number of their followers (i.e., the number of links or degree centrality for each node in an undirected network); random seeding ($s = 2$), which selects seeds randomly; and no seeding ($s = 3$), which does not involve seed selection. Although more sophisticated seeding strategies have been proposed in research (see Sect. 4.1.4), many are computationally expensive, making the aforementioned strategies more practical for implementation. In the case of either hub seeding or random seeding, the seeding rate (r) can be set in increments of 0.05, ranging from 0.05 to 0.50. The marketer may then select the value of r that optimizes profit for a given strategy. For the no-seeding strategy, r is defined as 0. By comparing the maximum profits achievable with these alternative strategies, the marketer can ultimately determine the optimal combination of seeding strategy and rate.

It is assumed that the total cost of seeding will increase proportionally with the number of targeted seeds and the unit costs associated with each seed, which are assumed to increase in proportion to the degree centrality of each seed. Let the overall fixed cost of seeding be designated as c_0. The variable cost is the sum of the unit costs imposed on the seeds, each of which is a linear combination of a constant term (κ) and a degree-dependent term proportional to a seed's degree with a coefficient of δ. Given a specified seeding strategy and rate (s, r) and a pair of cost conditions (κ, δ), the overall seeding cost can be calculated as follows:

$$C(s, r : \kappa, \delta, \boldsymbol{L}) = c_0 + \sum_{h \in \boldsymbol{Q}(s, r)} (\kappa + \delta L_h) \tag{4.1}$$

where $\boldsymbol{L} = (L_1, \ldots, L_M)$ is a vector of the degree centrality (L_h is the degree centrality or the number of followers of seed $h = 1, \ldots, M$) and $\boldsymbol{Q}(s, r)$ is a set of seeds selected given (s, r).

In this simulation, the parameter κ is set from 0.0 to 8.0 in increments of 1.0; the parameter δ is set from 0.000 to 0.030 in increments of 0.005. The revenue stream resulting from the seeding strategy, defined by parameters s and r, is converted to the NPV using a discount rate d (refer to 2.2.1 for a definition of this parameter). This value is denoted as NPV(s, r, d). Subsequently, the profit is calculated as the difference between the aforementioned NPV and the associated seeding cost, according to the following equation:

$$\Pi\left(s,r:d,\kappa,\delta,\boldsymbol{L}\right)=NPV\left(s,r,d\right)-C\left(s,r:\kappa,\delta,\boldsymbol{L}\right) \tag{4.2}$$

Assuming $c_0 = 0$ for simplicity, Eq. (4.2) is rewritten as:

$$\Pi\left(s,r,d:\kappa,\delta,\boldsymbol{L}\right)=NPV\left(s,r,d\right)-\sum_{h\in\boldsymbol{Q}(s,r)}\left(\kappa+\delta L_h\right) \tag{4.3}$$

The profit defined above depends on several additional simulation conditions, including external and internal factors related to the adoption process (π, θ), the mean and standard deviation of thresholds used in screening (μ, σ), the designation of the reference group in screening as either local or global (*ref*), and the network structure among potential adopters ($\boldsymbol{G}$). These simulation conditions are represented by vector o. The alternative levels of each component of o are set in accordance with the specifications outlined in Chap. 3 (Table 3.1). For hub seeding, each combination of alternative levels is selected once according to each agent's degree centrality, while for random seeding, the selection is repeated 20 times to avoid bias. Subsequently, for a given selection of seeds, the simulation is repeated 50 times. Each simulation consists of 1000 agents, and the time step is set from $t = 0$ to 100.

The calculation of profit for each seeding strategy is performed based on a combination of cost conditions (κ, δ) and simulation conditions o. Consequently, the seeding rate that maximizes profit for each strategy can be determined first. Then, the expected maximum profit of different seeding strategies, including no seeding, can be compared. Evidently, the seeding strategy that yields the highest expected profit represents the optimal approach. In the following section, we will examine how the optimal seeding strategy varies across the three scenarios, depending on differences in screening for adoption behavior.

4.2.2 Scenario of Weak Screening

As discussed in Chap. 3, the weak screening scenario is further subdivided into four subcases, each corresponding to different combinations of external and internal factors of adoption (π, θ). Tables 4.1, 4.2, 4.3, 4.4 present the optimal seeding strategies and projected profits across various network structures and cost conditions for the aforementioned subcases. The left half of each table displays the average seeding rate under the optimal strategy, while the right half shows the corresponding expected profit. The optimal seeding strategy is highlighted using color coding: pink cells indicate that hub seeding is the optimal strategy, while blue cells denote that random seeding is optimal. Uncolored cells signify that no seeding is optimal, whereas gray

Table 4.1 Optimal seeding in weak screening: $\pi = .01$ and $\theta = .10$

G	κ	Seeding rate							Profit						
		δ =							δ =						
		.000	.005	.010	.015	.020	.025	.030	.000	.005	.010	.015	.020	.025	.030
G2	0.0	1.00	.05	.05	.05	.00	.00	.00	1000	395	337	287	250	250	250
	1.0	.19	.05	.05	.00	.00	.00	.00	503	345	287	250	250	250	250
	2.0	.10	.05	.00	.00	.00	.00	.00	375	295	250	250	250	250	250
	3.0	.05	.00	.00	.00	.00	.00	.00	310	250	250	250	250	250	250
	4.0	.05	.00	.00	.00	.00	.00	.00	260	250	250	250	250	250	250
	5.0	.00	.00	.00	.00	.00	.00	.00	250	250	250	250	250	250	250
	6.0	.00	.00	.00	.00	.00	.00	.00	250	250	250	250	250	250	250
	7.0	.00	.00	.00	.00	.00	.00	.00	250	250	250	250	250	250	250
	8.0	.00	.00	.00	.00	.00	.00	.00	250	250	250	250	250	250	250
G4	0.0	1.00	.05	.05	.05	.00	.00	.00	1000	423	364	314	272	272	272
	1.0	.15	.05	.05	.00	.00	.00	.00	518	373	314	272	272	272	272
	2.0	.08	.05	.00	.00	.00	.00	.00	402	323	272	272	272	272	272
	3.0	.05	.05	.00	.00	.00	.00	.00	351	273	272	272	272	272	272
	4.0	.05	.00	.00	.00	.00	.00	.00	301	272	272	272	272	272	272
	5.0	.00	.00	.00	.00	.00	.00	.00	272	272	272	272	272	272	272
	6.0	.00	.00	.00	.00	.00	.00	.00	272	272	272	272	272	272	272
	7.0	.00	.00	.00	.00	.00	.00	.00	272	272	272	272	272	272	272
	8.0	.00	.00	.00	.00	.00	.00	.00	272	272	272	272	272	272	272
G6	0.0	1.00	.05	.05	.05	.00	.00	.00	1000	439	379	328	284	284	284
	1.0	.14	.05	.05	.00	.00	.00	.00	522	389	329	284	284	284	284
	2.0	.06	.05	.00	.00	.00	.00	.00	424	339	284	284	284	284	284
	3.0	.05	.05	.00	.00	.00	.00	.00	373	289	284	284	284	284	284
	4.0	.05	.00	.00	.00	.00	.00	.00	323	284	284	284	284	284	284
	5.0	.00	.00	.00	.00	.00	.00	.00	284	284	284	284	284	284	284
	6.0	.00	.00	.00	.00	.00	.00	.00	284	284	284	284	284	284	284
	7.0	.00	.00	.00	.00	.00	.00	.00	284	284	284	284	284	284	284
	8.0	.00	.00	.00	.00	.00	.00	.00	284	284	284	284	284	284	284
G8	0.0	1.00	.05	.05	.05	.00	.00	.00	1000	440	391	341	297	297	297
	1.0	.15	.05	.05	.00	.00	.00	.00	534	390	341	297	297	297	297
	2.0	.05	.05	.00	.00	.00	.00	.00	451	340	297	297	297	297	297
	3.0	.05	.00	.00	.00	.00	.00	.00	401	297	297	297	297	297	297
	4.0	.05	.00	.00	.00	.00	.00	.00	351	297	297	297	297	297	297
	5.0	.05	.00	.00	.00	.00	.00	.00	301	297	297	297	297	297	297
	6.0	.00	.00	.00	.00	.00	.00	.00	297	297	297	297	297	297	297
	7.0	.00	.00	.00	.00	.00	.00	.00	297	297	297	297	297	297	297
	8.0	.00	.00	.00	.00	.00	.00	.00	297	297	297	297	297	297	297
G10	0.0	1.00	.05	.05	.05	.00	.00	.00	1000	450	396	343	314	314	314
	1.0	.10	.05	.05	.00	.00	.00	.00	537	400	346	314	314	314	314
	2.0	.05	.05	.00	.00	.00	.00	.00	474	350	314	314	314	314	314
	3.0	.05	.00	.00	.00	.00	.00	.00	424	314	314	314	314	314	314
	4.0	.05	.00	.00	.00	.00	.00	.00	374	314	314	314	314	314	314
	5.0	.05	.00	.00	.00	.00	.00	.00	324	314	314	314	314	314	314
	6.0	.00	.00	.00	.00	.00	.00	.00	314	314	314	314	314	314	314
	7.0	.00	.00	.00	.00	.00	.00	.00	314	314	314	314	314	314	314
	8.0	.00	.00	.00	.00	.00	.00	.00	314	314	314	314	314	314	314

(pink) : Hub seeding is best; (blue) : Random seeding is best; Else: No seeding is best.

Note) κ: the constant of seeding cost per seed; δ: the degree-dependent cost; $d = 10\%$
G2, G4: small-world network; G6: random network;
G8: network with a log-normal degree distribution; G10: quasi-scale-free network.

Table 4.2 Optimal seeding in weak screening: $\pi = .01$ and $\theta = .05$

G	κ	Seeding rate δ = .000	.005	.010	.015	.020	.025	.030	Profit δ = .000	.005	.010	.015	.020	.025	.030
G2	0.0	1.00	.05	.05	.00	.00	.00	.00	1000	265	210	168	168	168	168
	1.0	.24	.05	.00	.00	.00	.00	.00	370	215	168	168	168	168	168
	2.0	.08	.00	.00	.00	.00	.00	.00	234	168	168	168	168	168	168
	3.0	.05	.00	.00	.00	.00	.00	.00	180	168	168	168	168	168	168
	4.0	.00	.00	.00	.00	.00	.00	.00	168	168	168	168	168	168	168
	5.0	.00	.00	.00	.00	.00	.00	.00	168	168	168	168	168	168	168
	6.0	.00	.00	.00	.00	.00	.00	.00	168	168	168	168	168	168	168
	7.0	.00	.00	.00	.00	.00	.00	.00	168	168	168	168	168	168	168
	8.0	.00	.00	.00	.00	.00	.00	.00	168	168	168	168	168	168	168
G4	0.0	1.00	.05	.05	.00	.00	.00	.00	1000	275	223	179	179	179	179
	1.0	.20	.05	.00	.00	.00	.00	.00	380	225	179	179	179	179	179
	2.0	.08	.00	.00	.00	.00	.00	.00	254	179	179	179	179	179	179
	3.0	.05	.00	.00	.00	.00	.00	.00	202	179	179	179	179	179	179
	4.0	.00	.00	.00	.00	.00	.00	.00	179	179	179	179	179	179	179
	5.0	.00	.00	.00	.00	.00	.00	.00	179	179	179	179	179	179	179
	6.0	.00	.00	.00	.00	.00	.00	.00	179	179	179	179	179	179	179
	7.0	.00	.00	.00	.00	.00	.00	.00	179	179	179	179	179	179	179
	8.0	.00	.00	.00	.00	.00	.00	.00	179	179	179	179	179	179	179
G6	0.0	1.00	.05	.05	.00	.00	.00	.00	1000	283	232	185	185	185	185
	1.0	.19	.05	.00	.00	.00	.00	.00	381	233	185	185	185	185	185
	2.0	.05	.00	.00	.00	.00	.00	.00	268	185	185	185	185	185	185
	3.0	.05	.00	.00	.00	.00	.00	.00	218	185	185	185	185	185	185
	4.0	.00	.00	.00	.00	.00	.00	.00	185	185	185	185	185	185	185
	5.0	.00	.00	.00	.00	.00	.00	.00	185	185	185	185	185	185	185
	6.0	.00	.00	.00	.00	.00	.00	.00	185	185	185	185	185	185	185
	7.0	.00	.00	.00	.00	.00	.00	.00	185	185	185	185	185	185	185
	8.0	.00	.00	.00	.00	.00	.00	.00	185	185	185	185	185	185	185
G8	0.0	1.00	.05	.05	.00	.00	.00	.00	1000	291	241	193	193	193	193
	1.0	.19	.05	.00	.00	.00	.00	.00	391	241	193	193	193	193	193
	2.0	.05	.00	.00	.00	.00	.00	.00	292	193	193	193	193	193	193
	3.0	.05	.00	.00	.00	.00	.00	.00	242	193	193	193	193	193	193
	4.0	.00	.00	.00	.00	.00	.00	.00	193	193	193	193	193	193	193
	5.0	.00	.00	.00	.00	.00	.00	.00	193	193	193	193	193	193	193
	6.0	.00	.00	.00	.00	.00	.00	.00	193	193	193	193	193	193	193
	7.0	.00	.00	.00	.00	.00	.00	.00	193	193	193	193	193	193	193
	8.0	.00	.00	.00	.00	.00	.00	.00	193	193	193	193	193	193	193
G10	0.0	1.00	.05	.05	.00	.00	.00	.00	1000	301	248	203	203	203	203
	1.0	.10	.05	.00	.00	.00	.00	.00	393	251	203	203	203	203	203
	2.0	.05	.00	.00	.00	.00	.00	.00	322	203	203	203	203	203	203
	3.0	.05	.00	.00	.00	.00	.00	.00	272	203	203	203	203	203	203
	4.0	.05	.00	.00	.00	.00	.00	.00	222	203	203	203	203	203	203
	5.0	.00	.00	.00	.00	.00	.00	.00	203	203	203	203	203	203	203
	6.0	.00	.00	.00	.00	.00	.00	.00	203	203	203	203	203	203	203
	7.0	.00	.00	.00	.00	.00	.00	.00	203	203	203	203	203	203	203
	8.0	.00	.00	.00	.00	.00	.00	.00	203	203	203	203	203	203	203

(pink) : Hub seeding is best; (blue) : Random seeding is best; Else: No seeding is best.

Note) κ: the constant of seeding cost per seed; δ: the degree-dependent cost; d = 10%
G2, G4: small-world network; G6: random network;
G8: network with a log-normal degree distribution; G10: quasi-scale-free network.

Table 4.3 Optimal seeding in weak screening: $\pi = .001$ and $\theta = .10$

G	κ	Seeding rate $\delta =$ .000	.005	.010	.015	.020	.025	.030	Profit $\delta =$ .000	.005	.010	.015	.020	.025	.030
G2	0.0	1.00	.05	.05	.05	.05	.05	.05	1000	324	259	203	153	103	53
	1.0	.20	.05	.05	.05	.05	.05	.00	479	274	209	153	103	53	50
	2.0	.10	.05	.05	.05	.05	.00	.00	335	224	159	103	53	50	50
	3.0	.06	.05	.05	.05	.00	.00	.00	241	174	109	53	50	50	50
	4.0	.05	.05	.05	.00	.00	.00	.00	189	124	59	50	50	50	50
	5.0	.05	.05	.00	.00	.00	.00	.00	139	74	50	50	50	50	50
	6.0	.05	.00	.00	.00	.00	.00	.00	89.3	50	50	50	50	50	50
	7.0	.00	.00	.00	.00	.00	.00	.00	49.9	50	50	50	50	50	50
	8.0	.00	.00	.00	.00	.00	.00	.00	49.9	50	50	50	50	50	50
G4	0.0	1.00	.05	.05	.05	.05	.05	.05	1000	372	299	248	197	147	96
	1.0	.20	.05	.05	.05	.05	.05	.00	499	322	249	198	147	97	72
	2.0	.10	.05	.05	.05	.05	.00	.00	370	272	199	148	97	72	72
	3.0	.05	.05	.05	.05	.00	.00	.00	299	222	149	98	72	72	72
	4.0	.05	.05	.05	.00	.00	.00	.00	249	172	99	72	72	72	72
	5.0	.05	.05	.00	.00	.00	.00	.00	199	122	72	72	72	72	72
	6.0	.05	.00	.00	.00	.00	.00	.00	149	72	72	72	72	72	72
	7.0	.05	.00	.00	.00	.00	.00	.00	99.2	72	72	72	72	72	72
	8.0	.00	.00	.00	.00	.00	.00	.00	72.4	72	72	72	72	72	72
G6	0.0	1.00	.05	.05	.05	.05	.05	.05	1000	397	321	270	220	169	119
	1.0	.16	.05	.05	.05	.05	.05	.00	506	347	271	220	170	119	83
	2.0	.08	.05	.05	.05	.05	.00	.00	389	297	221	170	120	83	83
	3.0	.05	.05	.05	.05	.00	.00	.00	331	247	171	120	83	83	83
	4.0	.05	.05	.05	.00	.00	.00	.00	281	197	121	83	83	83	83
	5.0	.05	.05	.00	.00	.00	.00	.00	231	147	83	83	83	83	83
	6.0	.05	.05	.00	.00	.00	.00	.00	181	97	83	83	83	83	83
	7.0	.05	.00	.00	.00	.00	.00	.00	131	83	83	83	83	83	83
	8.0	.00	.00	.00	.00	.00	.00	.00	83	83	83	83	83	83	83
G8	0.0	1.00	.05	.05	.05	.05	.05	.05	1000	400	341	292	243	193	144
	1.0	.15	.05	.05	.05	.05	.05	.00	517	350	291	242	193	143	105
	2.0	.06	.05	.05	.05	.05	.00	.00	418	300	241	192	143	105	105
	3.0	.05	.05	.05	.05	.00	.00	.00	367	250	191	142	105	105	105
	4.0	.05	.05	.05	.00	.00	.00	.00	317	200	141	105	105	105	105
	5.0	.05	.05	.00	.00	.00	.00	.00	267	150	105	105	105	105	105
	6.0	.05	.00	.00	.00	.00	.00	.00	217	105	105	105	105	105	105
	7.0	.05	.00	.00	.00	.00	.00	.00	167	105	105	105	105	105	105
	8.0	.05	.00	.00	.00	.00	.00	.00	117	105	105	105	105	105	105
G10	0.0	1.00	.05	.05	.05	.05	.05	.05	1000	411	358	304	251	198	144
	1.0	.10	.05	.05	.05	.05	.05	.00	518	361	308	254	201	148	135
	2.0	.05	.05	.05	.05	.05	.00	.00	449	311	258	204	151	135	135
	3.0	.05	.05	.05	.05	.00	.00	.00	399	261	208	154	135	135	135
	4.0	.05	.05	.05	.00	.00	.00	.00	349	211	158	135	135	135	135
	5.0	.05	.05	.00	.00	.00	.00	.00	299	161	135	135	135	135	135
	6.0	.05	.00	.00	.00	.00	.00	.00	249	135	135	135	135	135	135
	7.0	.05	.00	.00	.00	.00	.00	.00	199	135	135	135	135	135	135
	8.0	.05	.00	.00	.00	.00	.00	.00	149	135	135	135	135	135	135

(pink) : Hub seeding is best; (blue) : Random seeding is best; Else: No seeding is best.

Note) κ: the constant of seeding cost per seed; δ: the degree-dependent cost; $d = 10\%$
G2, G4: small-world network; G6: random network;
G8: network with a log-normal degree distribution; G10: quasi-scale-free network.

Table 4.4 Optimal seeding in weak screening: $\pi = .001$ and $\theta = .05$

G	κ	Seeding rate $\delta =$ .000	.005	.010	.015	.020	.025	.030	Profit $\delta =$ .000	.005	.010	.015	.020	.025	.030
G2	0.0	1.00	.05	.05	.05	.00	.00	.00	1000	171	109	59	22	22	22
	1.0	.26	.05	.05	.00	.00	.00	.00	341	121	59	22	22	22	22
	2.0	.11	.05	.00	.00	.00	.00	.00	170	71	22	22	22	22	22
	3.0	.05	.00	.00	.00	.00	.00	.00	86	22	22	22	22	22	22
	4.0	.05	.00	.00	.00	.00	.00	.00	36	22	22	22	22	22	22
	5.0	.00	.00	.00	.00	.00	.00	.00	22	22	22	22	22	22	22
	6.0	.00	.00	.00	.00	.00	.00	.00	22	22	22	22	22	22	22
	7.0	.00	.00	.00	.00	.00	.00	.00	22	22	22	22	22	22	22
	8.0	.00	.00	.00	.00	.00	.00	.00	22	22	22	22	22	22	22
G4	0.0	1.00	.05	.05	.05	.05	.00	.00	1000	196	132	82	31	27	27
	1.0	.25	.05	.05	.05	.00	.00	.00	351	146	82	32	27	27	27
	2.0	.10	.05	.05	.00	.00	.00	.00	195	96	32	27	27	27	27
	3.0	.05	.05	.00	.00	.00	.00	.00	123	46	27	27	27	27	27
	4.0	.05	.00	.00	.00	.00	.00	.00	73	27	27	27	27	27	27
	5.0	.00	.00	.00	.00	.00	.00	.00	27	27	27	27	27	27	27
	6.0	.00	.00	.00	.00	.00	.00	.00	27	27	27	27	27	27	27
	7.0	.00	.00	.00	.00	.00	.00	.00	27	27	27	27	27	27	27
	8.0	.00	.00	.00	.00	.00	.00	.00	27	27	27	27	27	27	27
G6	0.0	1.00	.05	.05	.05	.05	.00	.00	1000	213	146	96	46	30	30
	1.0	.25	.05	.05	.05	.00	.00	.00	352	163	96	46	30	30	30
	2.0	.10	.05	.05	.00	.00	.00	.00	212	113	46	30	30	30	30
	3.0	.05	.05	.00	.00	.00	.00	.00	148	63	30	30	30	30	30
	4.0	.05	.00	.00	.00	.00	.00	.00	98	30	30	30	30	30	30
	5.0	.05	.00	.00	.00	.00	.00	.00	48	30	30	30	30	30	30
	6.0	.00	.00	.00	.00	.00	.00	.00	30	30	30	30	30	30	30
	7.0	.00	.00	.00	.00	.00	.00	.00	30	30	30	30	30	30	30
	8.0	.00	.00	.00	.00	.00	.00	.00	30	30	30	30	30	30	30
G8	0.0	1.00	.05	.05	.05	.05	.00	.00	1000	217	165	116	66	39	39
	1.0	.20	.05	.05	.05	.00	.00	.00	362	167	115	66	39	39	39
	2.0	.08	.05	.05	.00	.00	.00	.00	240	117	65	39	39	39	39
	3.0	.05	.05	.00	.00	.00	.00	.00	184	67	39	39	39	39	39
	4.0	.05	.00	.00	.00	.00	.00	.00	134	39	39	39	39	39	39
	5.0	.05	.00	.00	.00	.00	.00	.00	84	39	39	39	39	39	39
	6.0	.00	.00	.00	.00	.00	.00	.00	39	39	39	39	39	39	39
	7.0	.00	.00	.00	.00	.00	.00	.00	39	39	39	39	39	39	39
	8.0	.00	.00	.00	.00	.00	.00	.00	39	39	39	39	39	39	39
G10	0.0	1.00	.05	.05	.05	.05	.00	.00	1000	238	185	131	78	53	53
	1.0	.11	.05	.05	.05	.00	.00	.00	359	188	135	81	53	53	53
	2.0	.05	.05	.05	.00	.00	.00	.00	276	138	85	53	53	53	53
	3.0	.05	.05	.00	.00	.00	.00	.00	226	88	53	53	53	53	53
	4.0	.05	.00	.00	.00	.00	.00	.00	176	53	53	53	53	53	53
	5.0	.05	.00	.00	.00	.00	.00	.00	126	53	53	53	53	53	53
	6.0	.05	.00	.00	.00	.00	.00	.00	76	53	53	53	53	53	53
	7.0	.00	.00	.00	.00	.00	.00	.00	53	53	53	53	53	53	53
	8.0	.00	.00	.00	.00	.00	.00	.00	53	53	53	53	53	53	53

(pink) : Hub seeding is best; (blue) : Random seeding is best; Else: No seeding is best.

Note) κ: the constant of seeding cost per seed; δ: the degree-dependent cost; d = 10%
G2, G4: small-world network; G6: random network;
G8: network with a log-normal degree distribution; G10: quasi-scale-free network.

cells indicate that a 100% seeding rate is optimal due to the absence of costs. The colored cells are henceforth referred to as the seeding-dominant cost region (SDCR).

In the scenario where screening is weak ($\mu = 0$), the subcase in which both the external and internal factors of adoption are strong ($\pi = 0.01$, $\theta = 0.10$) will be used as the baseline for subsequent comparisons. When cost conditions are fixed, the optimal strategy under these conditions can be determined; otherwise, it is necessary to identify the cost range that dominates seeding. As illustrated in Table 4.1, this range is constrained by both the constant and degree-dependent seeding costs (κ, δ). Clearly, if both costs are high, no seeding is the optimal strategy. Furthermore, the optimal seeding rate is 5% for most cost conditions, except in the cost-free condition, where the optimal seeding rate is 100%.

If only the internal factor is weakened compared to the aforementioned baseline subcase (i.e., if θ decreases from 0.10 to 0.05), as shown in Table 4.2, the SDCR contracts. This result aligns with the understanding that the internal adoption factor enhances the word-of-mouth effect. Consequently, it can be reasonably inferred that when this factor is weakened, the cost range within which seeding is recommended becomes narrower. Conversely, if the external factor is weakened (i.e., if π decreases from 0.01 to 0.001), the SDCR expands (Table 4.3). In other words, if the external factor is strengthened, diffusion will be facilitated even without seeding. This suggests the potential for a substitutional relationship between the external adoption factor and seeding interventions.

Ultimately, when both factors are diminished ($\pi = 0.001$, $\theta = 0.05$), as shown in Table 4.4, the SDCR expands compared to the baseline subcase (Table 4.1). However, this expansion is less pronounced than when only the external factor is weakened (Table 4.3). In other words, the weakening of the internal factor is believed to exert a slight countervailing effect (or negative synergy) on the impact of the weakening of the external factor.

An analysis of Tables 4.1, 4.2, 4.3, 4.4 reveals that when the network structure is G8 or G10, the cost range within which seeding is advantageous exhibits a slight expansion along the lambda axis. Determining whether this constitutes a significant change requires statistical analysis. Nevertheless, it appears that when selecting a seeding strategy that incorporates cost considerations, it is more prudent to prioritize the attributes of each agent's adoption behavior rather than the network structure between agents.

4.2.3 *Scenario of Strong Screening*

In the second scenario, screening is strong ($\mu = 0.1$), and the reference group is global. As outlined in subsection 3.2.3, this scenario is divided into four subcases based on the external factor of adoption (π) and the heterogeneity of the screening threshold (σ). The optimal seeding strategies under varying cost conditions for each subcase are presented in Tables 4.5, 4.6, 4.7, 4.8. To save space, only the results for G4 (small-world network) and G10 (quasi-scale-free network) are provided.

Table 4.5 Optimal seeding in strong screening with global references: $\pi = .01$ and $\sigma = .10$

		Seeding rate							Profit						
G	κ	$\delta =$ .000	.005	.010	.015	.020	.025	.030	$\delta =$ .000	.005	.010	.015	.020	.025	.030
G4	0.0	1.00	.10	.05	.05	.05	.00	.00	1000	245	180	129	79	56	56
	1.0	.20	.05	.05	.05	.00	.00	.00	440	186	130	79	56	56	56
	2.0	.13	.05	.05	.00	.00	.00	.00	277	136	80	56	56	56	56
	3.0	.10	.05	.00	.00	.00	.00	.00	176	86	56	56	56	56	56
	4.0	.05	.00	.00	.00	.00	.00	.00	113	56	56	56	56	56	56
	5.0	.05	.00	.00	.00	.00	.00	.00	63	56	56	56	56	56	56
	6.0	.00	.00	.00	.00	.00	.00	.00	56	56	56	56	56	56	56
	7.0	.00	.00	.00	.00	.00	.00	.00	56	56	56	56	56	56	56
	8.0	.00	.00	.00	.00	.00	.00	.00	56	56	56	56	56	56	56
G10	0.0	1.00	.08	.05	.05	.05	.00	.00	1000	258	201	148	94	68	68
	1.0	.15	.05	.05	.05	.00	.00	.00	440	204	151	98	68	68	68
	2.0	.10	.05	.05	.00	.00	.00	.00	322	154	101	68	68	68	68
	3.0	.05	.05	.00	.00	.00	.00	.00	245	104	68	68	68	68	68
	4.0	.05	.00	.00	.00	.00	.00	.00	195	68	68	68	68	68	68
	5.0	.05	.00	.00	.00	.00	.00	.00	145	68	68	68	68	68	68
	6.0	.05	.00	.00	.00	.00	.00	.00	95	68	68	68	68	68	68
	7.0	.00	.00	.00	.00	.00	.00	.00	68	68	68	68	68	68	68
	8.0	.00	.00	.00	.00	.00	.00	.00	68	68	68	68	68	68	68

: Hub seeding is best; : Random seeding is best; Else: No seeding is best.

Note) κ: the constant of seeding cost per seed; δ: the degree-dependent cost; $d = 10\%$
G4: small-world network; G10: quasi-scale-free network.

Table 4.6 Optimal seeding in strong screening with global references: $\pi = .01$ and $\sigma = .05$

		Seeding rate							Profit						
G	κ	$\delta =$ .000	.005	.010	.015	.020	.025	.030	$\delta =$ .000	.005	.010	.015	.020	.025	.030
G4	0.0	1.00	.10	.05	.05	.05	.00	.00	1000	267	143	93	42	3	3
	1.0	.20	.10	.05	.05	.00	.00	.00	451	167	93	43	3	3	3
	2.0	.10	.05	.05	.00	.00	.00	.00	299	105	43	3	3	3	3
	3.0	.10	.05	.00	.00	.00	.00	.00	199	55	3	3	3	3	3
	4.0	.10	.05	.00	.00	.00	.00	.00	99	5	3	3	3	3	3
	5.0	.10	.00	.00	.00	.00	.00	.00	32	3	3	3	3	3	3
	6.0	.00	.00	.00	.00	.00	.00	.00	3	3	3	3	3	3	3
	7.0	.00	.00	.00	.00	.00	.00	.00	3	3	3	3	3	3	3
	8.0	.00	.00	.00	.00	.00	.00	.00	3	3	3	3	3	3	3
G10	0.0	1.00	.10	.05	.05	.05	.00	.00	1000	276	161	108	55	3	3
	1.0	.15	.10	.05	.05	.05	.00	.00	453	176	111	58	5	3	3
	2.0	.10	.05	.05	.05	.00	.00	.00	339	115	61	8	3	3	3
	3.0	.10	.05	.05	.00	.00	.00	.00	239	65	11	3	3	3	3
	4.0	.05	.05	.00	.00	.00	.00	.00	167	15	3	3	3	3	3
	5.0	.05	.00	.00	.00	.00	.00	.00	117	3	3	3	3	3	3
	6.0	.05	.00	.00	.00	.00	.00	.00	67	3	3	3	3	3	3
	7.0	.05	.00	.00	.00	.00	.00	.00	17	3	3	3	3	3	3
	8.0	.00	.00	.00	.00	.00	.00	.00	3	3	3	3	3	3	3

: Hub seeding is best; : Random seeding is best; Else: No seeding is best.

Note) κ: the constant of seeding cost per seed; δ: the degree-dependent cost; $d = 10\%$
G4: small-world network; G10: quasi-scale-free network.

Table 4.7 Optimal seeding in strong screening with global references: $\pi = .001$ and $\sigma = .10$

G	κ	Seeding rate δ = .000	.005	.010	.015	.020	.025	.030	Profit δ = .000	.005	.010	.015	.020	.025	.030
G4	0.0	1.00	.10	.05	.05	.00	.00	.00	1000	183	88	38	3	3	3
	1.0	.25	.05	.05	.00	.00	.00	.00	420	111	38	3	3	3	3
	2.0	.13	.05	.00	.00	.00	.00	.00	237	61	3	3	3	3	3
	3.0	.10	.05	.00	.00	.00	.00	.00	130	11	3	3	3	3	3
	4.0	.10	.00	.00	.00	.00	.00	.00	42	3	3	3	3	3	3
	5.0	.00	.00	.00	.00	.00	.00	.00	3	3	3	3	3	3	3
	6.0	.00	.00	.00	.00	.00	.00	.00	3	3	3	3	3	3	3
	7.0	.00	.00	.00	.00	.00	.00	.00	3	3	3	3	3	3	3
	8.0	.00	.00	.00	.00	.00	.00	.00	3	3	3	3	3	3	3
G10	0.0	1.00	.10	.05	.05	.05	.00	.00	1000	209	132	79	25	4	4
	1.0	.15	.10	.05	.05	.00	.00	.00	415	135	82	29	4	4	4
	2.0	.10	.10	.05	.00	.00	.00	.00	292	85	32	4	4	4	4
	3.0	.05	.10	.00	.00	.00	.00	.00	204	35	4	4	4	4	4
	4.0	.05	.00	.00	.00	.00	.00	.00	154	4	4	4	4	4	4
	5.0	.05	.00	.00	.00	.00	.00	.00	104	4	4	4	4	4	4
	6.0	.05	.00	.00	.00	.00	.00	.00	54	4	4	4	4	4	4
	7.0	.05	.00	.00	.00	.00	.00	.00	4	4	4	4	4	4	4
	8.0	.00	.00	.00	.00	.00	.00	.00	4	4	4	4	4	4	4

(pink) : Hub seeding is best; (blue) : Random seeding is best; Else: No seeding is best.

Note) κ: the constant of seeding cost per seed; δ: the degree-dependent cost; $d = 10\%$
G4: small-world network; G10: quasi-scale-free network.

Table 4.8 Optimal seeding in strong screening with global references: $\pi = .001$ and $\sigma = .05$

G	κ	Seeding rate δ = .000	.005	.010	.015	.020	.025	.030	Profit δ = .000	.005	.010	.015	.020	.025	.030
G4	0.0	1.00	.10	.05	.05	.00	.00	.00	1000	207	54	3	0	0	0
	1.0	.23	.10	.05	.00	.00	.00	.00	422	107	4	0	0	0	0
	2.0	.15	.05	.00	.00	.00	.00	.00	255	25	0	0	0	0	0
	3.0	.10	.00	.00	.00	.00	.00	.00	146	0	0	0	0	0	0
	4.0	.10	.00	.00	.00	.00	.00	.00	46	0	0	0	0	0	0
	5.0	.00	.00	.00	.00	.00	.00	.00	0	0	0	0	0	0	0
	6.0	.00	.00	.00	.00	.00	.00	.00	0	0	0	0	0	0	0
	7.0	.00	.00	.00	.00	.00	.00	.00	0	0	0	0	0	0	0
	8.0	.00	.00	.00	.00	.00	.00	.00	0	0	0	0	0	0	0
G10	0.0	1.00	.10	.05	.05	.00	.00	.00	1000	232	86	32	0	0	0
	1.0	.15	.10	.05	.00	.00	.00	.00	428	132	36	0	0	0	0
	2.0	.10	.05	.00	.00	.00	.00	.00	308	50	0	0	0	0	0
	3.0	.10	.05	.00	.00	.00	.00	.00	208	0	0	0	0	0	0
	4.0	.05	.00	.00	.00	.00	.00	.00	125	0	0	0	0	0	0
	5.0	.05	.00	.00	.00	.00	.00	.00	75	0	0	0	0	0	0
	6.0	.05	.00	.00	.00	.00	.00	.00	25	0	0	0	0	0	0
	7.0	.00	.00	.00	.00	.00	.00	.00	0	0	0	0	0	0	0
	8.0	.00	.00	.00	.00	.00	.00	.00	0	0	0	0	0	0	0

(pink) : Hub seeding is best; (blue) : Random seeding is best; Else: No seeding is best.

Note) κ: the constant of seeding cost per seed; δ: the degree-dependent cost; $d = 10\%$
G4: small-world network; G10: quasi-scale-free network.

When only the external factor is weakened, the SDCR decreases slightly, which contrasts with the weak screening scenario. This suggests that strong screening with global references induces a positive complementary effect (or positive synergy) between the external factor and seeding. Furthermore, for quasi-scale-free networks, the SDCR expands in relation to the constant component of the unit cost of seeding (κ). Conversely, the effect of inter-agent heterogeneity in the screening threshold appears to be relatively minor.

Finally, the optimal seeding strategy is analyzed in the scenario of strong screening with local references (Tables 4.9, 4.10, 4.11, 4.12). As the external factor of adoption weakens, the SDCR expands slightly, similar to the previous scenario with a global reference. Therefore, it is hypothesized that a complementary effect with the external factor exists in strong screening, regardless of the reference group size. Furthermore, when the heterogeneity of the screening threshold (σ) is minimal, the SDCR expands. In this case, passing the screening becomes more challenging, but seeding helps to overcome this barrier and increase the number of initial adopters. This effect is more pronounced when the external factor is strong, reinforcing the presence of a complementary effect.

Table 4.13 facilitates comparison of the three scenarios by illustrating how the optimal seeding strategy varies depending on the scenario, network structure (G4 and G10), and behavioral parameters ($\{\pi, \theta\}$, or $\{\pi, \sigma\}$). In scenarios where the SDCR is significantly expanded, the following observations can be made:

Table 4.9 Optimal seeding in strong screening with global references: $\pi = .01$ and $\sigma = .10$

G	κ	Seeding rate							Profit						
		$\delta =$							$\delta =$						
		.000	.005	.010	.015	.020	.025	.030	.000	.005	.010	.015	.020	.025	.030
G4	0.0	1.00	.05	.05	.05	.05	.00	.00	1000	304	237	186	135	110	110
	1.0	.20	.05	.05	.05	.00	.00	.00	437	254	187	136	110	110	110
	2.0	.10	.05	.05	.00	.00	.00	.00	297	204	137	110	110	110	110
	3.0	.05	.05	.00	.00	.00	.00	.00	231	154	110	110	110	110	110
	4.0	.05	.00	.00	.00	.00	.00	.00	181	110	110	110	110	110	110
	5.0	.05	.00	.00	.00	.00	.00	.00	131	110	110	110	110	110	110
	6.0	.00	.00	.00	.00	.00	.00	.00	110	110	110	110	110	110	110
	7.0	.00	.00	.00	.00	.00	.00	.00	110	110	110	110	110	110	110
	8.0	.00	.00	.00	.00	.00	.00	.00	110	110	110	110	110	110	110
G10	0.0	1.00	.05	.05	.05	.05	.00	.00	1000	319	266	213	159	136	136
	1.0	.13	.05	.05	.05	.00	.00	.00	455	269	216	163	136	136	136
	2.0	.05	.05	.05	.00	.00	.00	.00	378	219	166	136	136	136	136
	3.0	.05	.05	.00	.00	.00	.00	.00	328	169	136	136	136	136	136
	4.0	.05	.00	.00	.00	.00	.00	.00	278	136	136	136	136	136	136
	5.0	.05	.00	.00	.00	.00	.00	.00	228	136	136	136	136	136	136
	6.0	.05	.00	.00	.00	.00	.00	.00	178	136	136	136	136	136	136
	7.0	.00	.00	.00	.00	.00	.00	.00	136	136	136	136	136	136	136
	8.0	.00	.00	.00	.00	.00	.00	.00	136	136	136	136	136	136	136

: Hub seeding is best; : Random seeding is best; Else: No seeding is best.

Note) κ: the constant of seeding cost per seed; δ: the degree-dependent cost; $d = 10\%$
G4: small-world network; G10: quasi-scale-free network.

Table 4.10 Optimal seeding in strong screening with global references: $\pi = .01$ and $\sigma = .05$

		Seeding rate							Profit						
G	κ	δ =							δ =						
		.000	.005	.010	.015	.020	.025	.030	.000	.005	.010	.015	.020	.025	.030
G4	0.0	1.00	.05	.05	.05	.05	.05	.00	1000	316	240	189	139	88	39
	1.0	.20	.05	.05	.05	.05	.00	.00	440	266	190	139	89	39	39
	2.0	.10	.05	.05	.05	.00	.00	.00	306	216	140	89	39	39	39
	3.0	.05	.05	.05	.05	.00	.00	.00	244	166	90	39	39	39	39
	4.0	.05	.05	.05	.00	.00	.00	.00	194	116	40	39	39	39	39
	5.0	.05	.05	.00	.00	.00	.00	.00	144	66	39	39	39	39	39
	6.0	.05	.00	.00	.00	.00	.00	.00	94	39	39	39	39	39	39
	7.0	.05	.00	.00	.00	.00	.00	.00	44	39	39	39	39	39	39
	8.0	.00	.00	.00	.00	.00	.00	.00	39	39	39	39	39	39	39
G10	0.0	1.00	.05	.05	.05	.05	.05	.05	1000	326	273	220	166	113	60
	1.0	.10	.05	.05	.05	.05	.05	.00	457	276	223	170	116	63	54
	2.0	.05	.05	.05	.05	.05	.00	.00	384	226	173	120	66	54	54
	3.0	.05	.05	.05	.05	.00	.00	.00	334	176	123	70	54	54	54
	4.0	.05	.05	.05	.00	.00	.00	.00	284	126	73	54	54	54	54
	5.0	.05	.05	.00	.00	.00	.00	.00	234	76	54	54	54	54	54
	6.0	.05	.00	.00	.00	.00	.00	.00	184	54	54	54	54	54	54
	7.0	.05	.00	.00	.00	.00	.00	.00	134	54	54	54	54	54	54
	8.0	.05	.00	.00	.00	.00	.00	.00	84	54	54	54	54	54	54

: Hub seeding is best; : Random seeding is best; Else: No seeding is best.

Note) κ: the constant of seeding cost per seed; δ: the degree-dependent cost; $d = 10\%$
G4: small-world network; G10: quasi-scale-free network.

Table 4.11 Optimal seeding in strong screening with local references: $\pi = .001$ and $\sigma = .10$

		Seeding rate							Profit						
G	κ	δ =							δ =						
		.000	.005	.010	.015	.020	.025	.030	.000	.005	.010	.015	.020	.025	.030
G4	0.0	1.00	.05	.05	.05	.05	.05	.00	1000	268	198	148	97	47	22
	1.0	.20	.05	.05	.05	.05	.00	.00	417	218	148	98	47	22	22
	2.0	.10	.05	.05	.05	.00	.00	.00	274	168	98	48	22	22	22
	3.0	.05	.05	.05	.00	.00	.00	.00	196	118	48	22	22	22	22
	4.0	.05	.05	.00	.00	.00	.00	.00	146	68	22	22	22	22	22
	5.0	.05	.00	.00	.00	.00	.00	.00	96	22	22	22	22	22	22
	6.0	.05	.00	.00	.00	.00	.00	.00	46	22	22	22	22	22	22
	7.0	.00	.00	.00	.00	.00	.00	.00	22	22	22	22	22	22	22
	8.0	.00	.00	.00	.00	.00	.00	.00	22	22	22	22	22	22	22
G10	0.0	1.00	.05	.05	.05	.05	.05	.00	1000	290	236	183	129	76	38
	1.0	.13	.05	.05	.05	.05	.00	.00	435	240	186	133	79	38	38
	2.0	.05	.05	.05	.05	.00	.00	.00	358	190	136	83	38	38	38
	3.0	.05	.05	.05	.00	.00	.00	.00	308	140	86	38	38	38	38
	4.0	.05	.05	.00	.00	.00	.00	.00	258	90	38	38	38	38	38
	5.0	.05	.05	.00	.00	.00	.00	.00	208	40	38	38	38	38	38
	6.0	.05	.00	.00	.00	.00	.00	.00	158	38	38	38	38	38	38
	7.0	.05	.00	.00	.00	.00	.00	.00	108	38	38	38	38	38	38
	8.0	.05	.00	.00	.00	.00	.00	.00	58	38	38	38	38	38	38

: Hub seeding is best; : Random seeding is best; Else: No seeding is best.

Note) κ: the constant of seeding cost per seed; δ: the degree-dependent cost; $d = 10\%$
G4: small-world network; G10: quasi-scale-free network.

Table 4.12 Optimal seeding in strong screening with local references: $\pi = .001$ and $\sigma = .05$

G	κ	Seeding rate							Profit						
		$\delta =$							$\delta =$						
		.000	.005	.010	.015	.020	.025	.030	.000	.005	.010	.015	.020	.025	.030
G4	0.0	1.00	.05	.05	.05	.05	.05	.05	1000	286	215	165	114	64	13
	1.0	.23	.05	.05	.05	.05	.05	.00	423	236	165	115	64	14	6
	2.0	.10	.05	.05	.05	.05	.00	.00	290	186	115	65	14	6	6
	3.0	.05	.05	.05	.05	.00	.00	.00	214	136	65	15	6	6	6
	4.0	.05	.05	.05	.00	.00	.00	.00	164	86	15	6	6	6	6
	5.0	.05	.05	.00	.00	.00	.00	.00	114	36	6	6	6	6	6
	6.0	.05	.00	.00	.00	.00	.00	.00	64	6	6	6	6	6	6
	7.0	.05	.00	.00	.00	.00	.00	.00	14	6	6	6	6	6	6
	8.0	.00	.00	.00	.00	.00	.00	.00	6	6	6	6	6	6	6
G10	0.0	1.00	.05	.05	.05	.05	.05	.05	1000	304	251	197	144	90	37
	1.0	.10	.05	.05	.05	.05	.05	.00	437	254	201	147	94	40	10
	2.0	.05	.05	.05	.05	.05	.00	.00	365	204	151	97	44	10	10
	3.0	.05	.05	.05	.05	.00	.00	.00	315	154	101	47	10	10	10
	4.0	.05	.05	.05	.00	.00	.00	.00	265	104	51	10	10	10	10
	5.0	.05	.05	.00	.00	.00	.00	.00	215	54	10	10	10	10	10
	6.0	.05	.00	.00	.00	.00	.00	.00	165	10	10	10	10	10	10
	7.0	.05	.00	.00	.00	.00	.00	.00	115	10	10	10	10	10	10
	8.0	.05	.00	.00	.00	.00	.00	.00	65	10	10	10	10	10	10

: Hub seeding is best; : Random seeding is best; Else: No seeding is best.

Note) κ: the constant of seeding cost per seed; δ: the degree-dependent cost; $d = 10\%$
G4: small-world network; G10: quasi-scale-free network.

1. Weak screening … When the external factor is weak and the internal factor is strong, the SDCR expands significantly. This suggests that seeding compensates for the weakness of external factors and is further accelerated by internal factors.
2. Strong screening with global references—The SDCR decreases; however, if a few hubs exist within the network, it expands to some extent.
3. Strong screening with local references—In cases where the external factor is relatively weak or the threshold heterogeneity is minimal, the SDCR becomes substantial. Conversely, if the external factor is strong and the threshold heterogeneity is large, the SDCR will decrease. In such cases, it may be more advantageous to forgo the expenditure on seeding.

In this study, two seeding strategies are considered: hub seeding and random seeding. The selection of the optimal strategy is determined by the seeding cost conditions, particularly the degree-dependent cost. In other words, as the degree-dependent cost increases, random seeding becomes more favorable.

4.2.4 Analysis of Robust Seeding Dominance

In the preceding section, we conducted a comparative analysis of the seeding-dominant range in terms of cost conditions and other parameters. A large seeding-dominant cost region (SDCR) indicates that seeding remains the dominant strategy

Table 4.13 Comparison of dominance of hub/random seeding

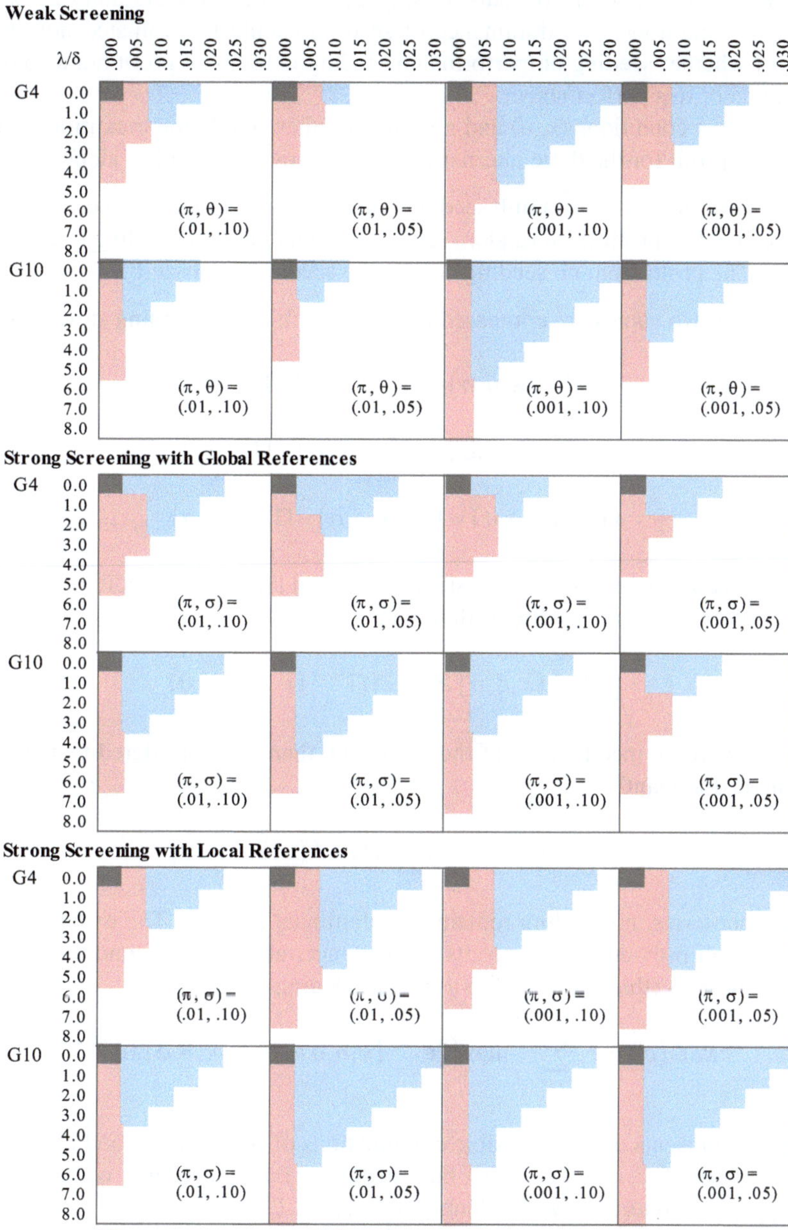

: Hub seeding is best; : Random seeding is best; Else: No seeding is best.

Note) λ: the constant of seeding cost per seed; δ: the degree-dependent cost;
G4: small-world network; G10: quasi-scale-free network; π, θ: the external/internal factor of adoption; σ: the heterogeneity of screening threshold

under different cost conditions, thereby demonstrating robustness. This robustness is a crucial consideration for marketers, given the inherent uncertainty associated with cost conditions. The dominance of seeding should be evaluated not only in terms of whether seeding outperforms no seeding in terms of profit but also by the magnitude of this performance.

Given cost conditions (κ, δ) and a vector of other simulation conditions ($\boldsymbol{o}$), the maximum profit for the three alternative seeding strategies can be calculated:

$\Pi^H(\kappa, \delta, \boldsymbol{o})$ = The profit from hub seeding with the optimal seeding rate.
$\Pi^R(\kappa, \delta, \boldsymbol{o})$ = The profit from random seeding with the optimal seeding rate.
$\Pi^N(\boldsymbol{o})$ = The profit from no seeding (where the seeding rate is zero).

and the first two values are compared from the profit across seeding strategies:

$$\Pi^{H-N}(\kappa,\delta,o) = \Pi^H(\kappa,\delta,o) - \Pi^N(o)$$

$$\Pi^{R-N}(\kappa,\delta,o) = \Pi^R(\kappa,\delta,o) - \Pi^N(o)$$

$$\Pi^{H-R}(\kappa,\delta,o) = \Pi^H(\kappa,\delta,o) - \Pi^R(\kappa,\delta,o)$$

If the subsequent conditional expression is satisfied for a given condition (κ, δ, $\boldsymbol{o}$), it is considered that "hub seeding is dominant":

$$\left(\Pi^{H-N}(\kappa,\delta,o) \geq 0\right) \& \left(\Pi^{H-R}(\kappa,\delta,o) \geq 0\right) \tag{4.4}$$

Conversely, if the inequality is of the following, then it is considered that "random seeding is dominant":

$$\left(\Pi^{R-N}(\kappa,\delta,o) \geq 0\right) \& \left(\Pi^{H-R}(\kappa,\delta,o) < 0\right) \tag{4.5}$$

In all other cases, no-seeding remains the dominant strategy. The extent to which seeding itself provides robust profits against uncertainty in cost conditions is measured as follows (this is referred to as robust seeding dominance):

$$RSD(o) = \sum_{(\kappa,\delta)\in D^S(o)} \max\left(\Pi^{H-N}(\kappa,\delta,o), \Pi^{R-N}(\kappa,\delta,o), 0\right) / |C| \tag{4.6}$$

where C represents a set of possible combinations of (κ, δ) values, and $D^S(\boldsymbol{o})$ represents a subset of C, in which either hub seeding or random seeding is the dominant strategy given conditions $\boldsymbol{o}$.[1] $|C|$ denotes the size of C.

RSD represents the expected value of the surplus profit generated by the optimal seeding strategy compared to the absence of seeding, assuming the prospective cost conditions remain uncertain, regardless of whether seeding is conducted at a hub or

[1] This set does not include the case of $\kappa = \delta = 0$ because seeding all agents is evidently optimal under such a cost condition.

through random selection. In cases where the cost conditions indicate that no seeding is more profitable, the surplus profit is assumed to be zero, as no seeding is undertaken. This value represents the expected surplus profit, assuming that all cost conditions within C have an equal probability of occurrence.

Furthermore, a measure of the advantage hub seeding holds over random or no seeding is introduced. This measure, termed robust hub seeding dominance, is computed as follows:

$$RHD(\boldsymbol{o}) = \sum_{(\kappa,\delta)\in D^H(o)} \Pi^H(\kappa,\delta,\boldsymbol{o}) / \left|D^S(\boldsymbol{o})\right| \tag{4.7}$$

where $D^H(\boldsymbol{o})$ represents a set of (κ, δ) values, in which hub seeding is the dominant strategy under conditions $\boldsymbol{o}$, and $|D^S(\boldsymbol{o})|$ indicates the number of cost condition combinations in which either hub seeding or random seeding is dominant given $\boldsymbol{o}$.

The next step is to analyze the relationship between RSD and RHD under different simulation conditions. The calculation of RSD and RHD assumes that profits from hub seeding, random seeding, and no seeding can be compared under identical simulation combinations. However, it should be noted that simulations for each seeding strategy are conducted independently. Furthermore, in parameter combinations, a single seed is selected for hub seeding, whereas multiple seeds are generated for random seeding. This raises the issue of how to align individual simulation trials across both strategies.

One potential solution is to average the measures for each combination of simulation conditions. However, this approach may not fully capture the inherent variability of simulation outcomes. Consequently, individual simulation trials for each strategy are randomly matched under a specific set of parameters. The resulting dataset contains as many cases as the number of parameter combinations multiplied by the number of iterations.

Figure 4.1 presents a scatter plot of RSD and RHD based on the aforementioned dataset. It reveals a strong correlation between the two variables. In other words,

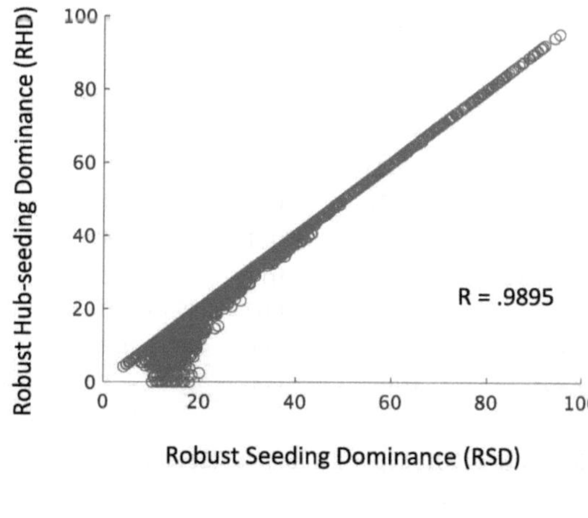

Fig. 4.1 Plots of robust seeding dominance and robust hub-seeding dominance

under simulation conditions where the cost domain favoring seeding is extensive, the cost domain favoring hub seeding also expands. This suggests that the choice between hub seeding and random seeding should primarily depend on cost conditions—particularly degree-dependent costs—rather than behavioral parameters or network structure.

In light of these findings, it is appropriate to analyze the regression results for RSD. The NPV used in profit calculations is based on a discount rate of $d = 10\%$. The independent variables include the main and interaction effects examined in Chap. 3, as well as interaction terms between the internal factor of adoption (θ) and network structure, as suggested by the preliminary analysis. The regression results in Table 4.14 highlight the following points:

1. Main Effects of Screening Scenarios: Using the weak screening scenario as a baseline, the cost region where seeding is dominant (RSD) shrinks in the strong screening scenario with the global reference group but expands in the scenario with the local reference group.

Table 4.14 Regression analysis on RSD with interaction terms: $d = 10\%$

		When weak			Shift to strong screening					
		Screening			w/ Global Ref.			w/ Local Ref.		
		Estimate	s.e.		Estimate	s.e.		Estimate	s.e.	
Const.		2.930	.007	s	−.162	.013	s	.204	.013	s
	G0	−.334	.010	s	.170	.017	s	−.056	.017	a
	G2	−.117	.010	s	.076	.017	s	−.066	.017	s
	G6	.102	.010	s	−.083	.017	s	.019	.017	
	G8	.070	.010	s	−.020	.017		.131	.017	s
	G10	.004	.010		.128	.017	s	.222	.017	s
π		−.911	.009	s	1.079	.016	s	1.002	.016	s
π	×G0	.281	.011	s	−.148	.019	s	−.232	.019	s
π	×G2	.100	.011	s	−.038	.019	b	−.108	.019	s
π	×G6	−.061	.011	s	.033	.019	c	−.011	.019	
π	×G8	−.032	.011	a	−.035	.019	s	−.073	.019	s
π	×G10	.008	.011		−.143	.019	s	−.117	.019	s
θ		.984	.009	s	−.259	.015	s	.172	.015	s
θ	×G0	−.071	.011	s	−.095	.019	s	−.088	.019	s
θ	×G2	−.004	.011		−.119	.019	s	.088	.019	s
θ	×G6	−.026	.011	b	.110	.019	s	−.007	.019	
θ	×G8	−.134	.011	s	.200	.019	s	−.060	.019	a
θ	×G10	−.319	.011	s	.319	.019	s	−.018	.019	
σ		−.044	.005	s	.057	.008	s	−.145	.008	s
$\pi \times \theta$		−.360	.006	s	.487	.011	s	.102	.011	s
$\pi \times \sigma$		.076	.006	s	−.390	.011	s	−.443	.011	s
					$N =$	9600		$R^2 =$	.969	

Note: s: $p < .001$; a: $p < .01$; b: $p < .05$; c: $p < .10$

2. Effect of Network Structure on RSD: The influence of network structure on RSD varies depending on the screening scenario. The only consistent observation is a positive effect for the quasi-scale-free network (G10). While many interaction terms involving network structure and other simulation conditions are statistically significant, they are too complex to be discussed in detail at this stage and will be addressed later.
3. Effect of External Adoption Factor (π): Under the weak screening scenario, the impact of π on RSD is negative, indicating a trade-off between seeding and external factors such as advertising or public relations. Conversely, in the strong screening scenarios, regardless of reference group coverage, the overall effect of π is slightly positive, suggesting a complementary or synergistic relationship between these factors.
4. Effect of Internal Adoption Factor (θ): In the weak screening scenario, the effect of θ on RSD is positive, indicating that RSD increases in conjunction with the influence of word-of-mouth propagation within networks. However, in the strong screening scenario with a global reference group, this effect is diminished. In contrast, when the reference group is local, the effect is amplified.
5. Effect of Screening Threshold Heterogeneity (σ): For weak screening, the impact of σ on RSD is negative, highlighting a trade-off with seeding. This trade-off intensifies in the strong screening scenario with local references but weakens when the reference group is global.

In order to compare the overall effects, including the interaction terms with the network structure, the predicted values of RSD for various combinations of simulation conditions were calculated. Figure 4.2a presents the predicted values for combinations of $\{\pi, \theta\}$ in the weak screening scenario, while Figs. 4.2b and c present predicted values for combinations of $\{\pi, \sigma\}$ in the strong screening scenarios, based on global or local reference groups. This classification is consistent with those in Chap. 3 and Sect. 4.2. However, the regression analysis conducted in the preceding section revealed that the interaction between the screening scenario and θ exerted a more pronounced influence on RSD compared to the interaction between θ and σ. Consequently, additional panels (4) and (5) have been included to illustrate the predicted values for combinations of $\{\pi, \theta\}$ in the strong screening scenario.

Figure 4.2a illustrates that, in the context of a weak screening scenario, the RSD is highest when the external factor (π) is relatively weak and the internal factor (θ) is strong. In this parameter combination, the NPV in the absence of seeding is relatively low (Fig. 3.6a), indicating that seeding is a highly recommended strategy. At this stage, seeding is considered an effective approach to mitigate the potential limitations of the external factor of adoption. However, it is crucial that the internal factor, which fosters word-of-mouth within the network, remains strong

In this case, the discrepancy attributable to network structure is less pronounced than that associated with the adoption behavior parameters. When the external factor is small and the internal factor is large, the RSD is the largest when the network structure is random. However, there is minimal difference under other combinations due to the network structure. If we recall that when seeding is not performed, the

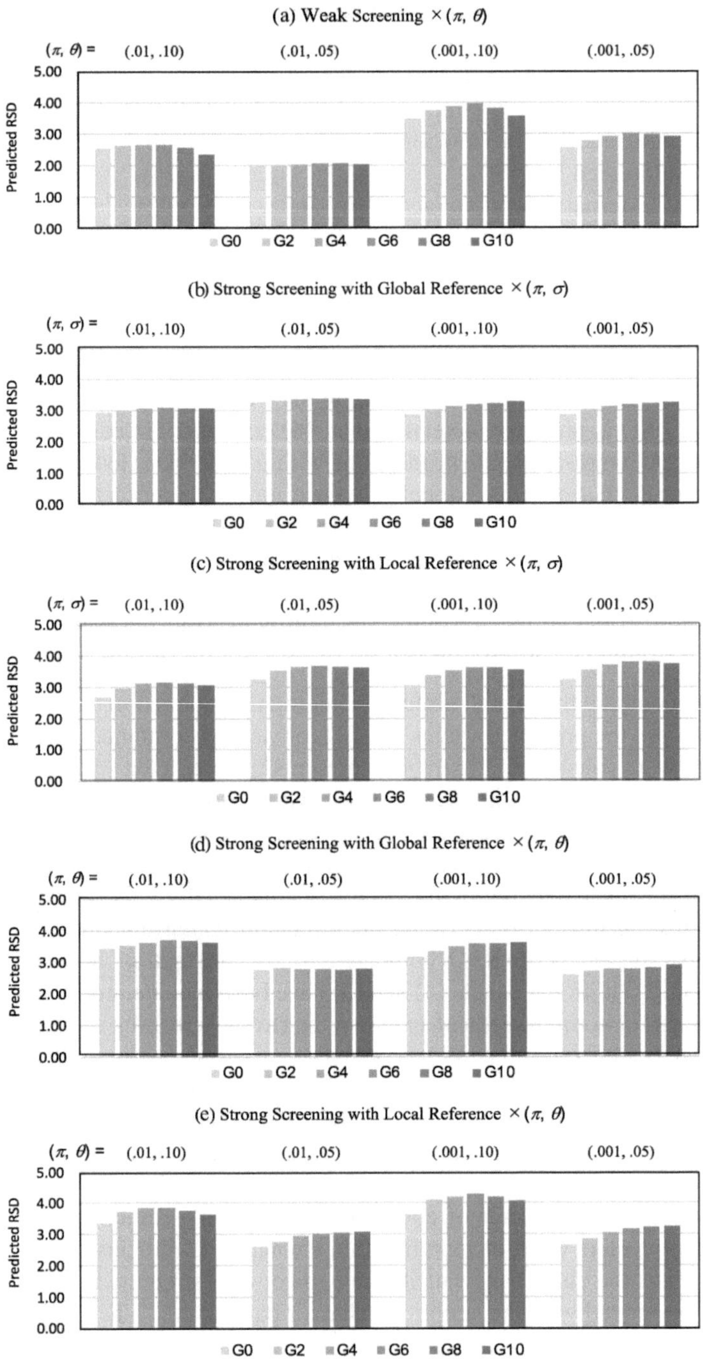

Fig. 4.2 Predicted values of RSD given simulation conditions when $d = 10\%$

NPV becomes larger the closer it is to a quasi-scale-free network (Fig. 3.6a), we can conclude that seeding has resolved the obstacles based on the network structure that originally existed.

In scenarios with strong screening, the distinction in RSD is more evident when considering combinations of $\{\pi, \theta\}$. Therefore, it is crucial to closely examine Figs. (d) and (e). Regardless of whether the reference group is global or local, the combination with a weak external factor and a strong internal factor exhibits the large RSD, as observed in (a). However, even in a combination where both external and internal factors are strong, the RSD is significantly larger than in other combinations. In the absence of seeding, the NPV for the former combination is markedly low, while for the latter combination it is positive. Consequently, seeding is more efficacious for the former combination, where external factors are weak and internal factors are strong.

The discrepancy in RSD resulting from variations in network structure is minimal for both (4) and (5), as it is for (1). Nevertheless, for certain combinations, RSD is marginally greater for specific network structures (as evidenced by the regression analysis in Table 4.14, this is a statistically significant difference).

4.3 Evaluating Seeding Strategies on Real-World Network

The evaluation framework for seeding strategies, as proposed in the previous section, will now be applied to a real-world setting. In order to achieve this, it is necessary to observe the process of influence propagation on social networks. This may be accomplished by monitoring the uptake of a new product on social media (e.g., [62, 68]). However, due to their vast number of users, social media networks are virtually limitless in scope, and their full connectedness is not readily captured by researchers outside the platform. With regard to its application to real-world influencer marketing, it is more efficient to commence with a potential influencer and subsequently investigate the surrounding network. To illustrate this approach, we present a study by Mizuno et al. [112].

4.3.1 Measuring the Ripple Effect of Social Media Post

Mizuno et al. [112] investigate the influence of influencers on their followers within a bipartite network structure on Twitter (now rebranded as X). They analyze the ripple effect of tweets (posts) on the same topic, focusing on the flow of information from influencers to their followers. In the Twitter network, reciprocal relationships between users are relatively rare, with only 22% observed in the study by Kwak et al. [94]. The flow of information and influence is primarily one-directional, as hubs with a large number of followers typically follow very few users in return. Even if they formally follow other users, their ability to engage with posts is likely limited. If potential influencers can be identified in advance, it becomes possible to analyze the diffusion of influence between them and their followers without being constrained to a specific community within the broader network.

A key limitation of focusing on the paths from influencers to followers is the inability to analyze the cascade phenomenon, in which information is transmitted from an influencer's immediate followers to their followers in multiple stages. While this presents a significant challenge, the computational cost of capturing all potential links within the network is prohibitively high, necessitating a compromise for practical feasibility. Another limitation is that the model disregards relationships between influencers, connections among followers, and feedback loops from followers to influencers, concentrating solely on the direct influence of influencers on their followers. This exclusion means that no attention is given to the broader interactions within the network. Given the complexity of estimating influence, this study restricts its focus to the direct influence exerted by influencers on their immediate followers. As a result, the proposed model cannot be classified as a traditional agent-based model, as interactions between agents are only partially considered. Nevertheless, it is introduced as a practical approach to seeding, incorporating seeding costs as discussed in the previous section.

Consider a bipartite network consisting of influencers ($i = 1, \ldots, I$) and their followers ($h = 1, \ldots, H$). The network contains $I \times H$ links, but estimating the strength of each individual influence is virtually impossible. Therefore, we calibrate the influence (η_i) for influencers ($i = 1, \ldots, I$) and susceptibility (β_h) for followers ($h = 1, \ldots, H$), capturing the relationship strength between influencers and followers as the product of these two factors. Based on this foundation, we formulate the following model for follower behavior. When an influencer posts about a specific product or brand, and that post is either retweeted or a new post on the same topic is created within a certain timeframe, it is considered that a ripple effect has occurred. We assume the probability that a follower h tweets about a product at time t ($y_{ht} = 1$ or 0) as a function of whether the influencers followed by h posted about the product within a given timeframe ($x_{hit} = 1$ or 0). This relationship is formulated using a binomial logit model as follows:

$$\Pr\left[y_{ht} = 1\right] = \frac{1}{1 + \exp\left(-\alpha_h - \beta_h \sum_{i=1}^{I} \eta_i x_{hit}\right)} \tag{4.8}$$

where the parameter α_h represents the inherent propensity of follower h to post on the same topic spontaneously. The binomial variable y_{ht} equals 1 if and only if follower h follows influencer i. It should be noted that the model assumes influencer posts occur exogenously and that the corresponding follower posts are independently generated among followers. The parameters $\boldsymbol{\alpha}$, $\boldsymbol{\beta}$, and $\boldsymbol{\eta}$ are calibrated under specific constraints to maximize the likelihood given the observed values of $\boldsymbol{x}$ and $\boldsymbol{y}$.

4.3.2 Data Collection and Model Calibration

This study utilized the Twitter API to collect Japanese-language posts published between November 8, 2011, and January 24, 2012, which contained the term "iPhone" (and its synonyms). A total of 4,865,284 posts were collected and used for parameter calibration. Additionally, 2,326,355 posts were gathered between March 1 and March 31, 2012, and utilized for model validation purposes. Among the 1,258,519 accounts included in both datasets, the 255 accounts that ranked within the top 1000 in terms of the number of retweets and the number of active days across both datasets were considered as influencers (their actual level of influence will be estimated at a later stage). Subsequently, accounts that were followed by these influencers were identified as followers. Finally, influencers and followers with sufficient posting frequency and links to calibrate the model were selected, resulting in a total of 160 influencers and 9874 followers.[2]

The calibration results for the parameters in Eq. (4.8) using these data are presented in Fig. 4.3 for influencers' influence (η), and in Fig. 4.4 for followers'

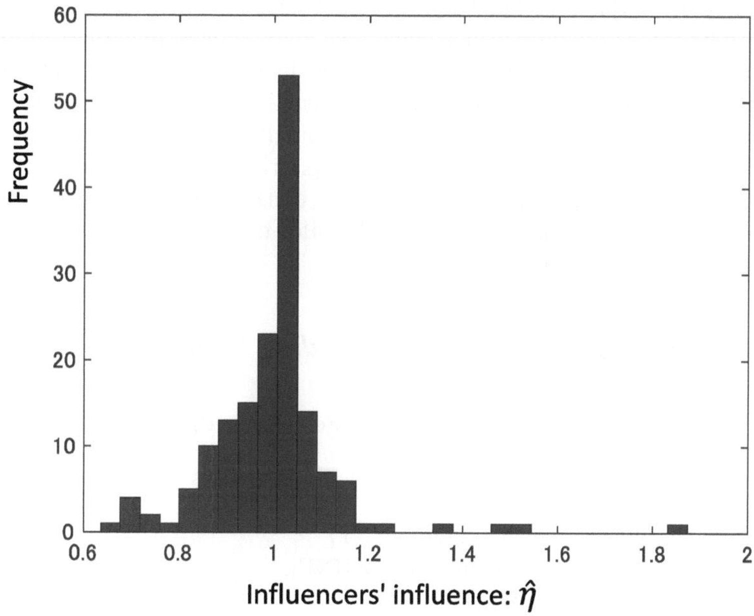

Fig. 4.3 Histogram of influence calibrated for influencers

[2]The network density between followers used in this analysis is 0.0007, indicating almost no connections. The network density among potential influencers is 0.0437, and the network density from followers to influencers is 0.0223, which is also highly sparse. Therefore, there is little direct influence between them, but there is the possibility of shared influence from mass media and other sources, so it cannot be said that there is no confounding relationship there. This process is a topic for future work.

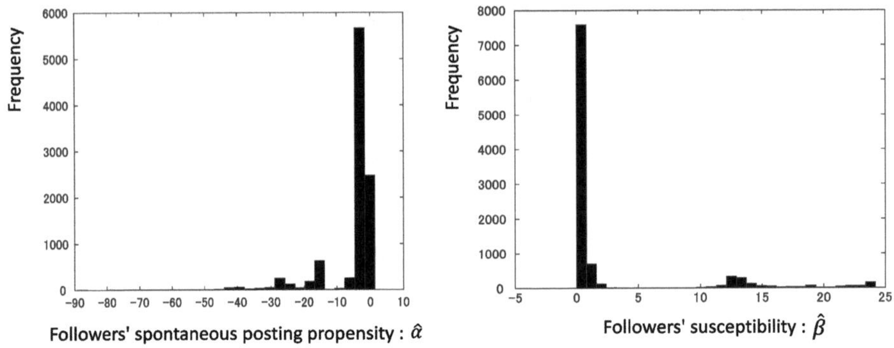

Fig. 4.4 Histogram of parameters calibrated for followers

spontaneous posting tendency ($\boldsymbol{\alpha}$) and susceptibility ($\boldsymbol{\beta}$). The influence calibrated for each influencer is unimodally distributed around 1, except for a few influencers who exhibit markedly elevated positive values. The spontaneous posting propensity calibrated for followers is categorized into two distinct groups: a small number with negative values and a large number with values near zero. The former corresponds to users who frequently propagate content related to iPhones, regardless of the most recent posts by the influencers they follow. The distribution of followers' susceptibility is polarized between near zero and significantly positive values, with the latter representing a minority. In other words, only a small number of followers are influenced by influencers to the extent of generating a ripple effect. From this perspective, seeding in influencer marketing should consider not only the number of followers but also the number of susceptible followers.

4.3.3 Comparison of Alternative Seeding Strategies

The following alternative seeding strategies are compared:

- Random seeding [RND].
- Hub seeding [HUB].
- Seeding based on number of retweets [RT].
- Seeding based on estimated influence, $\boldsymbol{\eta}$ [INF].
- Use of greedy algorithm [GRD].

The details of random seeding (RND) and hub seeding (HUB) were previously discussed in Sect. 4.2. The reasoning behind considering seeding based on the number of retweets (RT) is that the follower count observed on social media platforms may include inactive users. As a result, practitioners often use the number of retweets as a seeding criterion, as it serves as a measure of engagement. The use of estimated influence, $\boldsymbol{\eta}$ [INF], is a rational approach if this parameter can be calibrated. However, incorporating additional parameters could enable seeding to be performed using the following algorithm:

1. Suppose that seeding is conducted under strategy s and ratio r. The set of influencers chosen to seed the product is $\boldsymbol{Q}$ (consistent with 4.2). If all the influencers in $\boldsymbol{Q}$ simultaneously post about the product at once, the probability that their followers will post about the product within a specific period is calculated using Eq. (4.8) as follows:

$$\hat{p}(s,r) = \sum_{h=1}^{H} \frac{R_f\left(\sum_{i \in Q(s,r)} A_{hi}\,\hat{\theta}_i\right)}{H} \tag{4.9}$$

where A_{hi} is a binomial variable that is equal to 1 if follower h follows influencer i and is equal to 0 otherwise, and

$$R_h(z) = \frac{1}{1+\exp\left(-\hat{a}_h - \hat{\beta}_h\, z\right)}$$

2. The cost function for seeding is assumed to be identical to that presented in Eq. (4.1). It is further assumed that the gain from posting is directly proportional to the number of posts made by influencers and followers. Additionally, given that the propagation from influencer to follower is a one-time event, the expected gain from seeding can be calculated as follows:

$$\Pi(s,r) = I \cdot r + H \cdot \hat{p}(s,r) - C(s,r) \tag{4.10}$$

As assumed in Chap. 2, the average revenue per adopter is fixed at 1. Furthermore, for simplicity, we assume $c_0 = 0$. Equation (4.8) can then be rewritten as:

$$\Pi(s,r) = I \cdot r(1-\kappa) + H \cdot \hat{p}(s,r) - \delta \sum_{i \in Q(s,r)} L_i \tag{4.11}$$

where L_i is the degree centrality of influencer i.

3. It would be impractical to attempt every possible combination of seeds to maximize this function. Furthermore, it remains uncertain whether an algorithm exists that can efficiently solve this optimization problem. Therefore, a quasi-optimization approach is pursued through the following sequential computation:

(1) Compute the predicted contribution to profit if each influencer posts:

$$G_i(1) = \sum_{h=1}^{H} R_h\left(A_{hi}\,\hat{\eta}_i\right) - \left(\kappa + \delta L_i\right) \tag{4.12}$$

and select the influencer with the highest value as the first seed.

(2) Select the second seed from the remaining influencers using the same procedure, considering the tweets of the already selected seeds. This process is repeated until the given seed ratio (r) is reached. At each step, an influencer i (where $i \notin K_j$) that maximizes the following profit contribution is selected as the j-th seed:

$$G_i(j) = \sum_{h=1}^{H} R_f \left(A_{hi}\hat{\eta}_i + \sum_{k \in K_j} A_{hk}\hat{\eta}_k \right) - (\kappa + \delta L_i) \tag{4.13}$$

where K_j represents the set of seeds selected before the j-th seed.

Table 4.15 enumerates the best strategy and seed ratio under each cost condition. When the fixed cost per seed (κ) is relatively minimal, it is preferable to select influencers based on the influence level calibrated by the model rather than to seed 100% of the influencers, particularly when the degree-dependent cost (δ) increases slightly from zero. However, if δ increases further, the use of the greedy algorithm for seeding proposed in this study is most recommended. Nevertheless, if either κ or δ increases beyond a certain level, seeding becomes unprofitable regardless of the strategy used, and it is advisable to avoid seeding altogether.

Conversely, when the fixed cost per seed (κ) is relatively high (i.e., $\kappa > 1.0$) and the degree-dependent cost (δ) is close to zero, hub seeding is the preferred approach. In this case, the optimal seed ratio is inversely proportional to the value of κ. The size of the seed significantly impacts the overall cost, whereas the number of followers of the seed has a minimal impact. Consequently, it is optimal to select a seed with a high number of followers, as other information may be misleading. However, if the degree-dependent cost increases at this stage, the overall seeding cost will rise, leading to the conclusion that seeding should not be conducted.

4.4 Summary and Discussion

As social media has become more pervasive, influencer marketing has proliferated, and the question of who should be targeted as influencers, or "seeded," has garnered the attention of marketers. In Sect. 4.1, we provided an overview of the research on this topic, ranging from marketing science to computer science. One of the issues addressed in the aforementioned study is whether the hubs in the social network should be seeded or seeding should be done randomly (e.g., [166]). To address this question, we conducted a simulation that incorporated the seeding element into the agent-based diffusion model discussed in Sect. 4.3.

In considering the cost of seeding, companies aiming to spread new products are assumed to pursue profits by deducting the seeding cost from the NPV'. It is evident that the optimal seeding strategy for maximizing profits is contingent upon various cost conditions of seeding. We consider the cost conditions to be uncertain and seek a robust seeding strategy that generates high overall profits even when they vary.

Table 4.15 Comparison of dominance of alternative seeding strategies on real-world network

κ	$\delta=$ .00	.01	.02	.03	.04	.05	.10	.20	.30	.40	.50	.60	.70
.0	1.00	1.00	1.00	.50	.30	.25	.15	.10	.05	.05	.05	.05	.00
.1	1.00	1.00	.95	.50	.30	.25	.15	.10	.05	.05	.05	.00	.00
.2	1.00	1.00	.95	.50	.25	.20	.15	.05	.05	.05	.05	.00	.00
.3	1.00	1.00	.95	.50	.25	.20	.15	.05	.05	.05	.00	.00	.00
.4	1.00	1.00	.95	.50	.25	.20	.10	.05	.05	.00	.00	.00	.00
.5	1.00	1.00	.95	.30	.20	.15	.10	.05	.05	.00	.00	.00	.00
.6	1.00	1.00	.95	.30	.20	.15	.10	.05	.00	.00	.00	.00	.00
.7	1.00	1.00	.95	.05	.15	.15	.05	.05	.00	.00	.00	.00	.00
.8	1.00	1.00	.95	.05	.15	.10	.05	.00	.00	.00	.00	.00	.00
.9	1.00	1.00	.95	.05	.10	.05	.00	.00	.00	.00	.00	.00	.00
1.0	1.00	1.00	.95	.05	.00	.00	.00	.00	.00	.00	.00	.00	.00
2.0	.75	.70	.50	.00	.00	.00	.00	.00	.00	.00	.00	.00	.00
3.0	.65	.50	.05	.00	.00	.00	.00	.00	.00	.00	.00	.00	.00
4.0	.50	.45	.05	.00	.00	.00	.00	.00	.00	.00	.00	.00	.00
5.0	.50	.30	.05	.00	.00	.00	.00	.00	.00	.00	.00	.00	.00
6.0	.45	.20	.05	.00	.00	.00	.00	.00	.00	.00	.00	.00	.00
7.0	.35	.20	.05	.00	.00	.00	.00	.00	.00	.00	.00	.00	.00
8.0	.30	.05	.00	.00	.00	.00	.00	.00	.00	.00	.00	.00	.00
13.0	.10	.05	.00	.00	.00	.00	.00	.00	.00	.00	.00	.00	.00
14.0	.05	.05	.00	.00	.00	.00	.00	.00	.00	.00	.00	.00	.00
15.0	.05	.05	.00	.00	.00	.00	.00	.00	.00	.00	.00	.00	.00
19.0	.05	.05	.00	.00	.00	.00	.00	.00	.00	.00	.00	.00	.00
20.0	.05	.00	.00	.00	.00	.00	.00	.00	.00	.00	.00	.00	.00
30.0	.05	.00	.00	.00	.00	.00	.00	.00	.00	.00	.00	.00	.00
35.0	.00	.00	.00	.00	.00	.00	.00	.00	.00	.00	.00	.00	.00
40.0	.00	.00	.00	.00	.00	.00	.00	.00	.00	.00	.00	.00	.00

: GRD : HUB : RND : INF is best.

λ: the constant of seeding cost per seed; δ: the degree-dependent cost

In order to identify such a strategy, simulations are conducted in Sect. 4.2, where the conditions of adopter behavior and seeding costs are varied to ascertain the seeding-dominant cost region. The size of the cost region will depend on other simulation conditions, but whether hub seeding or random seeding will be dominant is largely determined by the degree-dependent cost. The lower this cost, the more dominant hub seeding will become.

The expected value of relative profit (robust seeding dominance, RSD) is calculated in the seeding-dominant cost region. The relationship between this value and other simulation conditions (network structures, adoption behaviors, etc.) is then analyzed. In scenarios where screening as a pre-adoption stage is weak (or practically absent), and where the external factor of adoption is weak while the internal factor is strong, the RSD becomes particularly large. This case is analogous to a situation where the influence of mass media advertising is relatively limited, yet the reach and persuasive power of word-of-mouth communication within a network is substantial. Furthermore, in this case, the NPV is markedly low when seeding is not implemented, thereby indicating that seeding has effectively mitigated such deficiencies. Additionally, in this context, the RSD is substantial in a network where each node is randomly connected to every other node (although the overall impact of the network structure is not particularly significant). In other words, the existence of a hub is relatively less important.

In the strong screening scenario, the impact of seeding on RSD is generally more significant than in the weak screening scenario, and the differences between the adoption behavior parameters are less significant. When seeding is not implemented, the NPV is minimal in many cases, indicating that strong screening hinders the diffusion of a new product. However, this limitation can be mitigated through seeding. The effect is particularly significant when the external factor of adoption is weak and the internal factor is strong. The differences in impact resulting from the network structure are less significant than in the weak screening scenario, yet they exhibit subtle variations depending on the parameter combination. In general, if the cost conditions fall within a specific range, seeding represents a reliable approach for enhancing profitability.

The challenge in applying this kind of framework to real-world situations lies in understanding the network of potential adopters. In Sect. 4.3, we quantify the ripple effect of posts on the bipartite network of influencers and followers observed on social media. Based on this analysis, we develop seeding strategies that incorporate the same seeding cost structure as previously described. In addition to the aforementioned straightforward strategies, such as hub seeding and random seeding, we also assess the profitability of a greedy algorithm based on a model derived from the propagation of information among potential adopters. The findings suggest that the proposed algorithm is more effective than other strategies when the degree-dependent cost is high.

When attempting to apply such a framework to a real-world scenario, the primary challenge lies in capturing the network of potential adopters. In Sect. 4.3, we extract the bipartite network between influencers and followers on social media, calibrate the ripple effect model of posts between them, and simulate seeding based on the same seeding cost structure as previously described. In addition to fundamental seeding strategies, such as hub seeding and random seeding, the comparison also includes a greedy algorithm based on the calibrated model. The results indicate that the proposed greedy algorithm is more effective than other strategies when the degree-dependent seeding cost is high.

The ripple effect model, as outlined in Sect. 4.3, is based on two key parameters: the influence of influencers and the susceptibility of followers. The GLM model, which has been the central focus of Chaps. 2, 3, 4, solely considers the latter aspect and, moreover, disregards the heterogeneity among agents. Figure 4.4 illustrates that there is considerable variation in susceptibility levels across individuals. It is also crucial to consider the heterogeneity of the influence of each agent. Expanding the GLM model in this direction is one of the promising avenues for future research. However, the studies discussed in Chap. 6 address the heterogeneity of influence and susceptibility in agents and the mechanisms by which they are generated.

Chapter 5
Empirical ABM for Marketing

A substantial number of studies have employed Agent-Based Modeling (ABM) with particular theoretical considerations, frequently exhibiting a lack of rigorous empirical foundation. To ensure the empirical validity of ABM, Rand and Rust [137] propose four crucial procedures: micro-face validation, macro-face validation, empirical input validation, and empirical output validation. The latter two procedures are particularly demanding in terms of methodology. Empirical input validation involves the utilization of real-world data to specify the behavior of individual agents, while empirical output validation entails the comparison of simulation outcomes with corresponding actual data at the aggregate level. Based on such discussions, this chapter presents two studies conducted by the author to contribute to the empirical validation of ABM.

5.1 Empirical ABM of New Product Diffusion and WOM

The introduction of an appealing new product gives rise to discussions among potential adopters with their peers, based on their experiences. These interactions can have a significant impact on the subsequent stages of new product diffusion. This section illustrates the application of empirical agent-based modeling (EABM) to analyze the diffusion of the iPhone in the Japanese mobile phone market. It considers the role of word-of-mouth (WOM) communication among potential adopters in fostering this diffusion.[1]

[1] This study represents a substantial modification and extension of the work by Mizuno et al. [115].

M. Mizuno, *Complex Modeling of Consumer Behavior*, Evolutionary Economics and Social Complexity Science 34,
https://doi.org/10.1007/978-4-431-54874-4_5

5.1.1 Questionnaire Surveys for Measuring New Product Adoption

By grasping the social networks among prospective adopters, it becomes possible to analyze the diffusion process with greater precision than would be possible through aggregate modeling, which lacks network information. An earlier study on new product diffusion examined social networks among physicians as potential adopters [37]. Extensive research on word-of-mouth in consumer behavior has actively pursued the measurement of offline social networks, particularly in studies such as Brown and Reingen [26] and Reingen et al. [140]. In recent years, the advent of social media has facilitated the measurement of expansive online networks among potential adopters and their behavior in adopting new products (e.g., [62, 68]).

Mizuno et al. [115] conducted an empirical study to observe the diffusion process of the iPhone 3G among employees of an engineering firm. The iPhone 3G, a smartphone introduced by Apple Inc., was first introduced to the Japanese market in July 2008, following its launch in other countries. This marked the first appearance of the iPhone in Japan, as the initial generation had only been available in the US market in 2007. Consequently, the iPhone was perceived as a highly innovative mobile phone by Japanese consumers at that time.

The study employed a web-based survey methodology, administered to a sample of employees from the Tokyo office of an engineering firm, which had an approximate workforce of 500 individuals. The majority of employees in this firm demonstrated a greater familiarity with high-tech products than workers in other industries. The initial survey was conducted between July 30 and August 20, 2008, shortly after the launch of the iPhone 3G. A total of 180 employees responded to the initial survey, yielding a response rate of 35%. The second survey was conducted for the same group of respondents from October 21 to 29, 3 months after the initial survey. Among the participants in the first survey, 132 employees responded to the second survey, achieving a response rate of 73%.

The questionnaires utilized in both surveys were nearly identical and requested information from respondents regarding their awareness, knowledge, purchase consideration/experience (adoption), and frequency of discussions about the iPhone 3G within the firm, as well as their personal attributes. It is noteworthy that the majority of respondents were male (approximately 80%) and aged between 20 and 39 (70% or higher). Additionally, a significant proportion of respondents identified as engineers (approximately 80%).

In the initial survey, the adoption rate of the iPhone 3G was 2.2%, while in the subsequent survey, it increased to 5.5%. It is noteworthy that the surveys were conducted during a period when the iPhone 3G was exclusively offered by SoftBank, one of the mobile phone carriers in Japan. It is unlikely that users of alternative carriers, even if they found the iPhone attractive, would have been willing to incur the costs associated with changing carriers. Subsequently, another carrier, Au, began offering the iPhone series in 2011, followed by Docomo, the largest carrier in the market, in 2013. At present, the iPhone has become the most popular brand in the Japanese mobile phone market.

Nevertheless, the adoption rate at that time appears to have been insufficient for accurately predicting the results of the diffusion model utilized in this study. Consequently, purchase consideration, which was one of the variables measured in the aforementioned surveys, is employed as a proxy variable for adoption. With this redefinition, the "adoption rate" was 31.8% in the initial survey and 42.6% in the subsequent survey. It is crucial to recognize that the differentiation between adoption (purchase) and purchase consideration is not merely contingent on behavioral or attitudinal elements; it also encompasses the concept of irreversibility or reversibility. In practice, 5.4% of respondents who initially indicated purchase consideration in the initial survey changed their attitudes in the subsequent survey. However, this study assumes that respondents who expressed purchase consideration in the initial survey would maintain this attitude over time, given that adoption is considered an irreversible decision.

5.1.2 Constructing Word-of-Mouth (WOM) Networks Based on Surveys

In the surveys conducted, each respondent was asked to recall up to ten colleagues with whom they had engaged in conversation about the iPhone 3G up to that point. Although these relationships are inherently directed, for simplicity, they were converted into undirected connections. If at least one of the two respondents recalled a conversation between them, they were considered linked in the undirected network. Two WOM networks were constructed using the valid responses from the first and second surveys, respectively, as illustrated in Fig. 5.1.

The networks consist of numerous isolated nodes, defined as respondents who did not interact with anyone about the new iPhone product, and several connected components, defined as respondents who interacted with a limited number of peers.

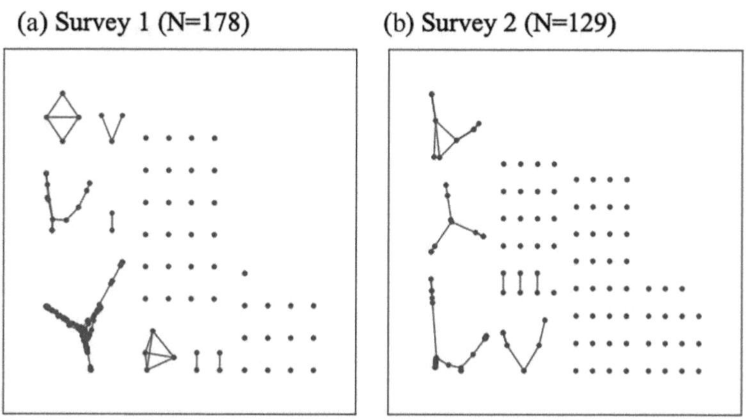

Fig. 5.1 WOM networks constructed based on the two surveys

Table 5.1 presents the distribution of component sizes between the initial and subsequent surveys. In the initial survey, approximately 80% of respondents were affiliated with one of the eight connected components, each with at least one node, and 62.9% were part of the largest component. In the second survey, approximately 50% of respondents belonged to one of the seven connected components, with 26.4% being part of the largest connected component (see Fig. 5.2). Between the two surveys, the number of isolated nodes increased, and there was a weakening of concentration in the largest component, possibly indicating a decline in interest toward the new product.

The degree distributions of the four WOM networks are illustrated in Fig. 5.3. The figures depict the degree distributions of (a) the entire network in the first survey, (b) the entire network in the second survey, (c) the 1 maximal connected

Table 5.1 Component size distributions of WOM networks

	The first survey				The second survey			
Component size	N	%	# nodes	%	N	%	# nodes	%
1	37	82.2	37	20.8	64	90.1	64	49.6
2	3	6.7	6	3.4	3	4.2	6	4.7
3	1	2.2	3	1.7	0	0.0	0	0.0
4	2	4.4	8	4.5	0	0.0	0	0.0
6	0	0.0	0	0.0	1	1.4	6	4.7
9	0	0.0	0	0.0	1	1.4	9	7.0
10	0	0.0	0	0.0	1	1.4	10	7.8
12	1	2.2	12	6.7	0	0.0	0	0.0
34	0	0.0	0	0.0	1	1.4	34	26.4
112	1	2.2	112	62.9	0	0.0	0	0.0
Total	45	100.0	178	100.0	71	100.0	129	100.0

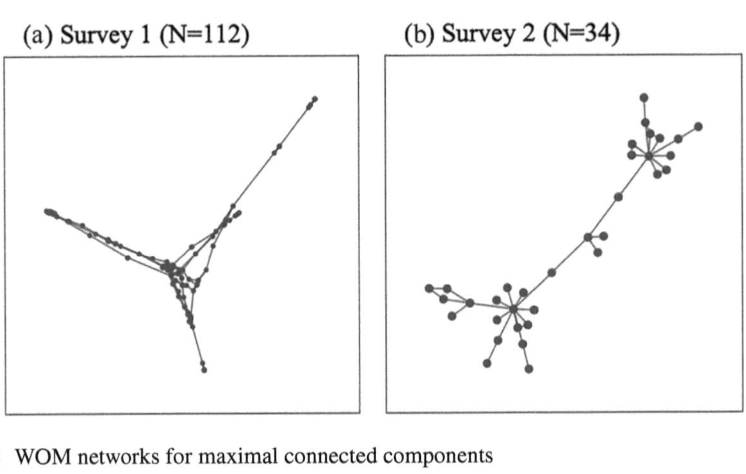

Fig. 5.2 WOM networks for maximal connected components

component in the first survey, and (d) the largest connected component in the second survey. The distributions indicate that a significant proportion of respondents engage in conversations about the new product with only a few colleagues, while a smaller number of respondents participate in conversations with a larger number of colleagues. It is important to note that the survey imposed a limit of ten conversation partners, which may have influenced the reported numbers. It is possible that some respondents engaged with a larger number of people than reported. Given the limited size of the dataset, it is challenging to identify the precise type of distribution with certainty. However, it is evident that the distribution exhibits a long-tail nature. Figures 5.3 (b) and (d) illustrate the degree distributions of the largest connected components. As anticipated, nodes with relatively high degrees are present within this component.

When the network properties were calculated specifically for the largest connected component, the average distance and clustering coefficient were found to be 5.575 and 0.418 for the network from the first survey, and 4.279 and 0.386 for the network from the second survey, respectively. These findings indicate that both networks display attributes of a small-world network. The network derived from the initial survey is employed as the primary network in the simulation.

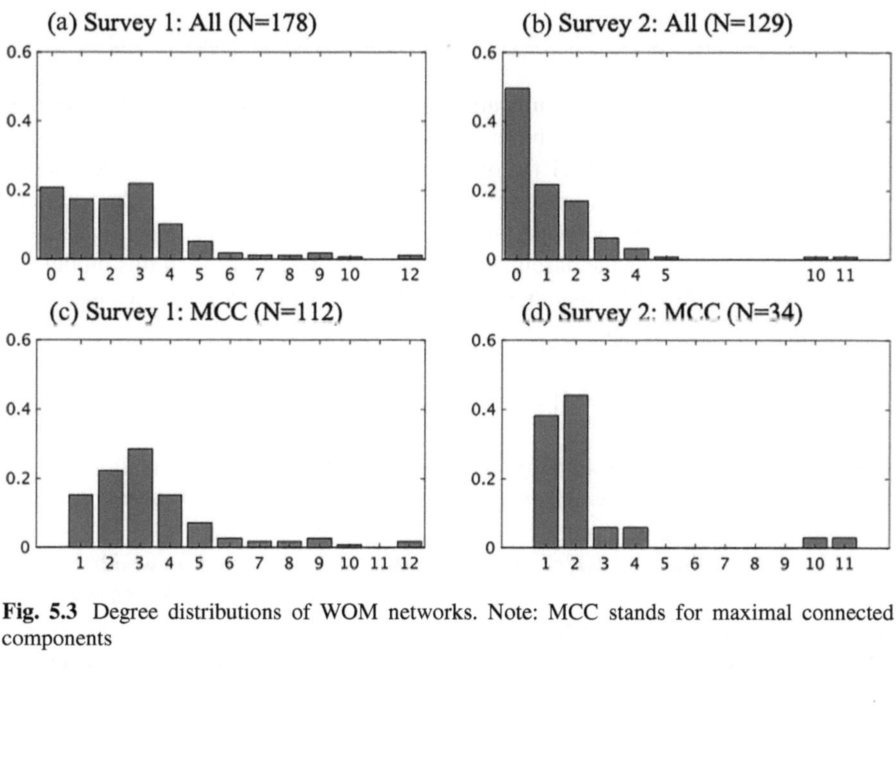

Fig. 5.3 Degree distributions of WOM networks. Note: MCC stands for maximal connected components

5.1.3 Modeling New Product Adoption and WOM Generation

In this study, the calibration process ensures empirical input validation, as defined by Rand and Rust [137], through the initialization of the agents and the network based on the data obtained from the initial survey. Empirical output validation is achieved by minimizing the discrepancy between the resulting macro- and micro-states of the simulation and the data from the second survey, with respect to the model parameters. This is accomplished through a grid search technique that incorporates regression tree methods, which are a form of machine learning. Further details of the calibration process are provided below.

The model of new product adoption is primarily based on the formulation of the GLM model (Eq. 2.2 in Chap. 2). The probability of adoption for agent $h = 1, \ldots, H$ at time $t = 1, \ldots, T$, given that they have not yet adopted the focal product, is formulated as follows:

$$\Pr\left[x_{ht} = 1 | x_{h\tau} = 0, \tau < t\right] = 1 - (1 - \pi) \prod_{k \neq h} (1 - \theta)^{x_{h,t-1} y_{hkt}} \tag{5.1}$$

where $x_{ht} = 1$ if agent h has adopted the product by time t; $x_{ht} = 0$, otherwise,

π: The probability that an agent adopts it due to the external factor such as advertising,

θ: The probability that an agent adopts it due to the internal factor, which is the influence from another agent who has already adopted it,

$y_{hkt} = 1$ if agents h and k have a conversation about the product at time t; $y_{hkt} = 0$, otherwise.

In this model, WOM communication on the focal product between agents is endogenous and influenced by both external and internal factors, as well as new product adoption. The internal factor pertains to conversations aimed at sharing information based on the experience of purchasing and using the product. Conversely, the external factor pertains to conversations arising from a variety of other reasons, serving as the baseline for conversation generation in this model.

The overall probability that a pair of agents will engage in a conversation (generation of WOM) is formulated as follows:

$$\Pr\left[y_{hkt} = 1\right] = 1 - (1 - \psi_{hk})(1 - \zeta)^{\max(x_{h,t-1}, x_{k,t-1})} \tag{5.2}$$

where ψ_{hk}: The baseline probability that agents h and k have a conversation,

ζ: The probability that two agents have a conversation as a result of at least either of the pair adopting a new product.

This model defines a network of WOM communication based on whether agents engage in conversations about the product, which generates WOM. Moreover, it evolves over time in accordance with the diffusion process. It is important to note that the interactions among agents within this WOM-generated network are not necessarily irreversible, unlike the adoption process. Links that exist at a given point in time may disappear in the subsequent period. At the individual level, adopting a new product and interacting with others are mutually reinforcing. At the aggregate level, the diffusion of the product and the WOM network coevolve.

5.1.4 Simulation for Calibrating the Agent-Based Model

The parameters to be calibrated are as follows:

$\pi \in [0, 1)$: The probability of the product adoption by the external factor,
$\theta \in [0, 1)$: The probability of the product adoption by the internal factor,
$\psi_{hk} \in [0, 1)$: The baseline probability of chat between agents h and k,
$\zeta \in [0, 1)$: The probability of WOM generation if at least either of agents already adopted a new product.

In order to assess the empirical input validity of the proposed approach, the agents in the above model are matched with valid respondents in the two surveys. To perform the simulation under the constraints of data availability, ψ_{hk} is substituted by $\psi \cdot y_{hk0}$, where y_{hk0} is a dummy variable representing the initial connectivity between agents h and k, taking 1 if both agents are linked in the initial network based on the first survey and $\psi \in [0, 1)$. If a set of alternative values for the aforementioned parameters is provided, the simulation is conducted in accordance with the following procedure:

1. Determine the initial adoption of agent h, denoted as x_{h0} ($h = 1, \ldots, H$), based on the response obtained from the initial survey. In addition, determine the conversation experience between agent h and k, y_{hk0}, based on the aforementioned network. Let $t = 1$.
2. Calculate the probabilities of WOM communication between all pairs of agents using Eq. (5.2) based on the previous state of adoption $\{x_{h,t-1}, x_{k,t-1}\}$. Following these, determine whether pair $\{h, k\}$ has a conversation or not (i.e., $y_{hkt} = 1$ or 0) at time t.
3. Calculate the probabilities that the agents who have not adopted yet (i.e., $x_{h,t-1} = 0$) will do so using Eq. (5.1) and determine whether each agent adopt the new product or not. (i.e., $x_{ht} = 1$ or 0).
4. If $t < T$, let $t + 1 \to t$ and return to step 2. Otherwise, stop the process. T is the final time period of the simulation.

In each simulation for calibration, the time horizon is set to $T = 15$, which is the number of weeks between the two surveys. This simulation is iterated N times for each combination of parameter values. At time T in the n-th iteration, the adoption state of agent h is documented as $x_{hT}^{(n)}$, while the interaction between h and k is documented as $y_{hkT}^{(n)}$. Both are binomial variables taking 0 or 1. The value of T is fixed at a predetermined level.

5.1.5 Goodness of Fit of the Simulated Outcomes

The actual data utilized for comparison with the individual-level predictions encompass the respondent's adoption of the product, denoted as X_h, and the interaction between respondents h and k, denoted as Y_{hk}. These variables are based on valid responses from the second survey. As previously stated, the adoption variable is derived from the stated purchase consideration data, which has been modified to be irreversible. The interaction variable is derived from the stated conversation experience data, which has been adjusted for symmetry. Both variables are dichotomized as binomial variables, taking values of 0 or 1. Aggregating these variables across all respondents provides the actual diffusion rate and network density as aggregate-level outcomes.

The goodness of fit of the model is assessed by calculating the inverse of the deviance between the model predictions and the actual data from the second survey. Deviance indices for adoption and interaction are calculated at both the aggregate- and disaggregate-levels as follows:

The aggregate-level deviance index of adoption.:

$$Dev(\boldsymbol{x}) = \left| \sum_{n=1}^{N} \sum_{h=1}^{H} x_{hT}^{(n)} / N - \sum_{h=1}^{H} X_h \right| / H \tag{5.3}$$

The aggregate-level deviance index of interaction:

$$Dev(\boldsymbol{y}) = \left| \sum_{n=1}^{N} \sum_{h=1}^{H} \sum_{k \neq h} y_{hkT}^{(n)} / N - \sum_{h=1}^{H} \sum_{k \neq h} Y_{hk} \right| / \left(\frac{N \cdot H(H-1)}{2} \right) \tag{5.4}$$

The disaggregate-level deviance index of adoption:

$$dev(\boldsymbol{x}) = \sum_{h=1}^{H} \left| \sum_{n=1}^{N} x_{hT}^{(n)} / N - X_h \right| / H \tag{5.5}$$

The disaggregate-level deviance index of interaction:

$$dev(\boldsymbol{y}) = \sum_{h=1}^{H} \sum_{k \neq h} \left| \sum_{n=1}^{N} y_{hkT}^{(n)} / N - Y_{hk} \right| / \left(\frac{H(H-1)}{2} \right) \tag{5.6}$$

Since the diffusion of a new product is a macro phenomenon, it is important to consider deviance at the aggregate level when evaluating the validity of the model. However, in order to fine-tune the parameter values, it is also necessary to consider deviance at the disaggregate (individual) level. Therefore, all deviance indices are standardized and simply summed to form the overall deviance index. This index serves as an objective function to be minimized with respect to the parameters $\{\pi, \theta, \psi, \zeta\}$.

5.1.6 *Iterated Calibration Procedure and Results*

The approach of this study to minimize the overall deviance index, as an objective function, involves sequential iterations of regression tree analysis, a widely used machine learning technique. The methodology's distinctive feature is its implementation of simulations for all potential combinations of parameter values, similar to a grid search. Upon identification of a relatively optimal range of parameter values through regression tree analysis, these values are further subdivided, resulting in a series of combinations for subsequent simulation steps. This process is then repeated with another round of regression tree analysis. This strategy may prove a viable alternative to the grid search in calibrating ABM to empirical data.

The utility of grid search is enhanced by its capacity to accommodate objectives that are either non-differentiable or mathematically intricate. Nevertheless, it may present a computational challenge when dealing with a substantial number of alternative parameter values. A further disadvantage is the lack of information on the obtained optimal value. Given the potentially vast number of parameter value combinations, the data size corresponding to a single combination is unavoidably restricted, which results in lower reliability of the discovered "point estimates"by grid search. Conversely, regression tree analysis searches for intervals where the objective function approximates its optimal value, which offers some assurance regarding parameter reliability.

Another advantage of regression tree analysis is its efficiency in identifying interactions specific to nonlinear systems, as demonstrated in Sect. 3.2. This characteristic is absent in linear regression models, which are the predominant methods used in statistical analysis. In this research, the Classification and Regression Tree (CART) method was employed for regression tree analysis. To ensure the validity of the results, each parameter was assigned a theoretical bound of [0, 1). Initially, this bound was divided into ten discrete levels, ranging from 0 to 0.9 in increments of 0.1. All possible combinations of these levels were generated, resulting in a total of 10,040 cases. To enhance result reliability, simulations were iterated ten times for each combination, generating simulated data.

The simulated data underwent regression tree analysis to identify parameter value intervals that minimized the overall deviance index. Table 5.2 provides a summary of this process. The "Option 0" row represents the initial parameter value bounds in the first round, while subsequent rows illustrate alternative partitions of the parameter values. The partitions are ordered according to the resulting overall deviance. The "Selected" column indicates the partition chosen as the optimal solution in each round. The union of these selected partitions formed the initial bounds for each parameter value in the subsequent round. Each bound was further divided into multiple discrete levels, and all possible combinations of these levels were generated. Regression tree analysis was then reapplied to partition the simulation results based on the updated conditions.

In the second round, Table 5.3 demonstrates that only one partition exhibited a superior overall deviance index relative to the others, thereby establishing this

Table 5.2 The process of exploring the best parameter values (Round 1)

Option	π	θ	ψ	ζ	Deviance	Selected
0	[0, .9] by .1	[0, .9] by .1	[0, .9] by .1	[0, .9] by .1		
1	[0, .05)	[.15, .15)	[0, .05)	[0, .05)	−19.858	x
2	[0, .05)	[.15, .35)	[0, .05)	[0, .05)	−19.809	x
3	[0, .05)	[0, .05)		[0, .05)	−19.805	x
4	[0, .05)	[0, .05)		[.05, .15)	−19.451	
5	[0, .05)	[0, .05)		[.15, .25)	−19.076	

Note: Option 0 is the initial bounds of parameter values; Options 1 to 5: top five partitions in terms of the overall deviance

Table 5.3 The process of exploring the best parameter values (Round 2)

Option	π	θ	ψ	ζ	Deviance	Select
0	[0, .1] by .02	[0, .4] by .1	[0, .9] by .02	[0, .1] by .02		
1	[0, .01)	[.05, .25)	[0, .05)	[0, .01)	−20.148	x
2	[0, .01)	[0, .05)		[0, .03)	−19.779	
3	[0, .01)	[0, .05)		[.03, .05	−19.677	
4	[0, .01)	[0, .05)		[.05, .09)	−19.565	
5	[0, .01)	[0, .05)		0.09	−19.452	

partition as the optimal solution. This process of partitioning was then repeated until the fourth round, at which point no further partition resulted in a reduction in the overall deviance index.

Tables 5.4 and 5.5 provide a comprehensive account of the detailed steps and outcomes of this iterative procedure. The final selected partition is $\{\pi \in [0, .00375), \theta \in [.125, .135), \psi \in [.045, .05), \zeta \in [0, .00125)\}$, where the parameter values are interpreted as follows:

1. The final selected range of π, which is nearly zero, indicates that the impact of the external factor of adoption can be disregarded to enhance the model's parsimony. This calibration outcome is interpreted as the initial value for adoption, x_{h0}, already accounting for the effect of external factors.
2. The selected range of θ, which spans from 0.125 to 0.135, indicates that the internal factor exerts a considerable influence on the adoption process. It is therefore valuable to incorporate the WOM network into the micro-level diffusion model, as this allows for the effective capture of the effects of interactions among individuals.
3. The selected range of ψ, which spans from 0.045 to 0.05, represents a small but non-zero probability that individuals who had a conversation about the new product shortly after its launch will engage in another conversation about it at a later point in time. This implies that conversations about the new product persist among both adopters and non-adopters, and continue to stimulate new adoption.
4. The selected range of ζ, which is nearly zero, indicates that the parameter of adoption-led conversation can be disregarded. The results suggest that discussions about new products occur independently of new product adoption, highlighting the role of organic conversation among individuals.

Table 5.4 The process of exploring the best parameter values (Round 3)

Option	π	θ	ψ	ζ	Deviance	Select
0	[0, .01] y .005	[0, .25] by .01	[0, .05] by .01	[0, .01] by .005		
1	[0, .0025)	[.105, .135)	[0, .05)	[0, .0025)	−20.029	x
2	[0, .0075)	[.05, .105)	[0, .035)	[0, .0025)	−20.005	x
3	[0, .0025)	[.135, .185)	[0, .045)	[0, .0025)	−19.957	
4	[0, .0075)	[.05, .105)	[.035, .05)	[0, .0025)	−19.953	
5	[0, .0075)	[.185, .25)	[0, .005)	[0, .0025)	−19.942	

Table 5.5 The process of exploring the best parameter values (Round 4)

Option	π	θ	ψ	ζ	Deviance	Selected
0	0 or .0075	[.05, .135] by .01	[0, .05] by .01	0 or .0025		
1	[0, .00375)	[.125, .135)	[.045, .05)	[0, .00125)	−20.234	x
2	[0, .00375)	[.105, .115)	[.045, .05)	[0, .00125)	−20.226	
3	[0, .00375)	[.05, .055)	[0, .005)	[.00125, .0025)	−20.214	
4	[0, .00375)	[.075, .105)	[.045, .05)	[0, .00125)	−20.129	
5	[0, .00375)	[.105, .115)	[.005, .045)	[0, .00125)	−20.129	

The findings of this study indicate that the parameter of the external factor of adoption (π) and the adoption-led conversation parameter (ζ) are nearly zero. Consequently, the model can be simplified to two parameters: θ, which represents the probability of adoption via conversations with adopters (internal effect), and ψ, which indicates the likelihood of repeated conversations.

5.1.7 *Sensitivity Analysis of the Calibrated Model*

The outcomes of the aforementioned calibration may be excessively influenced by the methodology employed in the calibration of the data and parameters utilized to fit the model. The reliability of the outcomes can be evaluated through an examination of the results of the sensitivity analysis, specifically by determining the extent to which the model output is altered when the calibrated parameter is subject to slight modifications. In other words, if the model output exhibits minimal variation, it can be deemed to possess a robust character.

The calibrated values of the model parameters are $(\pi, \theta, \psi, \zeta) = (.00, .13, .0475, .00)$, and alternative levels are created by increasing or decreasing each parameter by .025 (or .05). However, if the resulting value is negative, it is excluded. The simulation should be repeated 100 times for each combination, resulting in a total of 1600 repetitions. The results of the simulation should be evaluated using the NPV generated by the diffusion model. It should be assumed that the discount rate is 10% and that one adoption generates a profit of 1.

Table 5.6 presents the results of the regression model, which comprises the main effects of the parameters and the two-way interactions, estimated for the NPV

Table 5.6 Regression analysis on NPV with interactions

	.025-point change			.05-point change		
	estimate	s.e.		estimate	s.e.	
Const.	37.6	21.7	c	40.1	0.5	s
π	652.0	93.8	s	606.7	11.1	s
θ	100.8	182.0		71.9	4.9	s
ψ	110.0	469.5		30.6	11.6	a
ζ	1112.2	93.8	s	1065.3	11.1	s
$\pi \times \theta$	−812.0	196.5	s	−766.9	97.3	s
$\pi \times \psi$	−1145.4	1964.9		−33.9	102.4	
$\theta \times \psi$	−645.6	3929.8		102.4	102.4	
$\pi \times \zeta$	−9051.7	98.2	s	−9282.4	97.3	s
$\theta \times \zeta$	974.8	196.5	s	1368.2	97.3	s
$\psi \times \zeta$	−888.0	1964.9		−783.3	102.4	s
N	1600			1600		
R^2	.991			.991		

Note: s: $p < .001$; a: $p < .01$; b: $p < .05$; c: $p < .10$

obtained from the aforementioned simulation. First, when the range of variation of the parameters is 0.025, the main effects of π and ζ, as well as the interactions of $\theta \times \zeta$, $\pi \times \theta$, and $\pi \times \zeta$, are statistically significant. In other words, the calibrated values of π and ζ, which are close to zero, have the potential to significantly alter the results of the diffusion if they are only slightly positive. Therefore, it is recommended that these parameters be set to zero in order to better fit the observed data. If the range of variation for the parameters is set to 0.05, the main effects of θ and ψ, and the interaction of $\psi \times \zeta$, become significant. Therefore, it seems preferable to maintain the current values for θ and ψ.

The calibrated model may also be used to derive strategic implications based on the results of the sensitivity analysis. This is to say that if the results exhibit a notable improvement when the parameter values undergo slight alterations, it is possible to contemplate strategies that modify the parameters that have been fixed during calibration.

a. A slight increase in either the external factor of adoption (π) or the spread of information by adopters (ζ) will result in a notable enhancement of NPV. However, since there is a significant negative interaction between these two parameters, it is of the utmost importance for the marketer to prioritize the promotion of either one.
b. The internal factor (θ) of adoption and the baseline probability (ψ) of conversion will significantly enhance the NPV if the increase is substantial. Even if the increase is modest, there is a positive interaction between these two parameters, indicating that augmenting both will enhance the NPV.

As is evident, the results presented above are largely limited by the data collected in this study. Had we been able to obtain a larger sample from a more diverse population, we might have been able to obtain results with greater generalizability. Nevertheless, even if we could observe the networks between consumers on a large scale on social media, it is generally difficult to capture their consumption behaviors. Conversely, even if we could obtain a substantial amount of individual purchase history data, it is generally difficult to capture the networks between individuals. This problem represents a significant challenge in analyzing the diffusion of new products using EABM.

5.2 Another Example: TV Program Viewing Model

To present another example of empirical agent-based modeling (EABM), we present a brief summary of Mizuno and Nishiyama [116], modeling individual-level television viewing behaviors with social interaction. It employs a massive dataset of television viewing data for academic research, which is commercially provided for advertising management. The availability of such data allows data analysts to obtain reliable statistical estimations of the parameters of individual-level models. However, information about interactions among agents (i.e., the network) is scarce in comparison to the preceding section, where networks among agents were measured by questionnaire surveys. Fortunately, this data contains a limited amount of information on social interaction, such as household membership. Additionally, we can construct hypothetical networks among agents and check their validity. This study suggests that the increasing prevalence of big data would expand the applicability of EABM in a wider area of marketing research.

5.2.1 Modeling Program Choice Behavior in TV Viewing

Television viewing behavior can be modeled as a two-stage choice process, where the decision to engage with television is made first, followed by the choice of channel or broadcast station. Rust et al. [145] formulated the initial stage using a binomial logit choice model and the subsequent stage using a multinomial logit choice model. These discrete choice models have been extensively utilized across a range of fields, including marketing, civil engineering, and applied econometrics (see, for instance, [16, 72, 105, 106]). The initial stage can be regarded as a choice among various potential activities or, alternatively, as a routine action. If the viewer chooses to watch television at a specific time, the subsequent analysis will focus on the viewer's decision regarding the channels and programs to watch.

The choice of a channel or program is likely influenced by viewers' content preferences, habitual patterns, and social influences from peers or reference groups. The probability of a viewer choosing a particular channel can be expressed through the following multinomial logit model:

$$\Pr\left(y_{hit}=1\right)=\exp\left(\boldsymbol{\alpha}_h\boldsymbol{x}_{hit}\right)/\sum_{j\in C}\exp\left(\boldsymbol{\alpha}_h\boldsymbol{x}_{hjt}\right) \tag{5.7}$$

where $\boldsymbol{x}_{hit}$ represents a vector of attribute values that channel i has at time t, that may vary among viewers as will be described below; $\boldsymbol{\alpha}_h$, on the other hand, represents a vector of preferences for each attribute. It is well established that this choice probability follows from the assumption that agent h chooses an option from the choice set $\{1, \ldots, i, \ldots, I\}$ that maximizes the following utility function:

$$u_{hit}=\boldsymbol{\alpha}_h\boldsymbol{x}_{hit}+\varepsilon_{hit} \tag{5.8}$$

where ε_{hit} is assumed to be independently and identically type-I extreme-value distributed [105].

In this research, the attribute vector, $\boldsymbol{x}$, is formulated as follows:

1. Program Position: Coordinates in the program space of a channel (program), aired during the current time slot.
2. Viewing Inertia: Whether the viewer had been watching the same channel immediately before the current time slot.
3. Viewing Habits: Whether the viewer had watched the same channel during the same time slot in the previous week.
4. Intra-Family Influence: Whether another family member had been watching the same channel during the current time slot.
5. Gender-Age Influence: The channel ratings during the same time slot in the previous week for viewers within the same gender-age group.
6. Homophilic Influence: The channel ratings during the same time slot in the previous week for viewers in the same neighborhood in the program space.

The first and sixth attributes, program position and homophilic influence, are determined by the program space, in which programs are organized based on similarities in viewer composition. To construct this, a viewer-program matrix is created by counting the frequency with which each viewer selects a channel. This matrix is then subjected to the multidimensional scaling technique to calculate the coordinates of each program within a two-dimensional space. These coordinates are then utilized as attribute values for program position.

By employing the share of viewing time by each viewer over programs as a weight to calculate the average coordinates of the program, it is possible to derive the coordinates of viewers within the same space. This results in the formation of a "neighborhood" of viewers within a specific radius of one another within the program space, reflecting a convergence of similar preferences. It is proposed that the decisions of each viewer are influenced by the viewing behaviors of their neighbors. For an illustrative explanation of the program space, refer to Fig. 5.4.

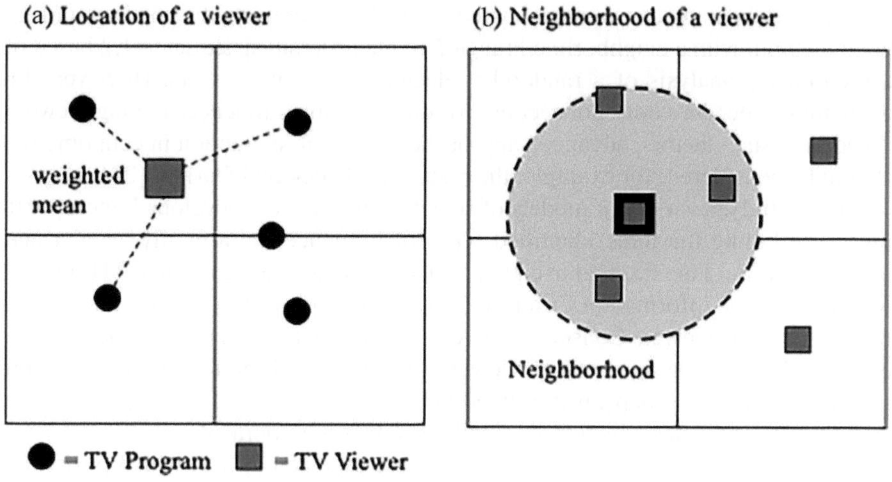

Fig. 5.4 Illustrative explanation of program space

5.2.2 Calibrating Virtually Networked Individual Models

The behavior of television viewers at the individual level has been automatically and longitudinally measured in panel households through the use of a special electronic device attached to a television set. This study employs data from the aforementioned panel households, which are profiled as follows:

- Sample: 1963 viewers from 500 households in the Kanto area of Japan (including cities such as Tokyo and Yokohama).
- Time Period: From January to March 2000, with the exception of the first week of January, which featured numerous special programs.
- Channel: One public broadcasting station (NHK) and five private stations in the Japanese TV network, excluding the NHK educational station.
- Program: Major programs aired during prime time (7:00 p.m. to 11:00 p.m.), excluding special programs, with each assigned a 30 minute time slot.

It is important to note that the data were collected from family members residing in the same household, thereby providing information that could be used to infer the potential influence of intra-family dynamics.

In applying the discrete choice model to data related to television viewing, it is crucial to identify the specific channel selected by the viewer during a given time slot. However, viewing time data are inherently continuous. Consequently, it is assumed that viewers select a channel if they spend the majority of their time on that channel during a given time slot, provided that the viewing duration is at least 10 min. To ensure the reliability of individual-level estimates, a sample of 1766 viewers was selected, excluding those who watched television for less than 50 min during the period.

The model parameters were estimated for each viewer using the maximum likelihood method, with a neighborhood range L in the program space set to 1.2 based on a preliminary analysis of a randomly selected 1% of all viewers. However, this estimation procedure does not account for unobservable influences among viewers. To address such factors, advanced approaches to social interaction in econometrics should be considered, for example, the studies by Brock and Durlauf [23].

In this study, a variety of models of social influence were developed, incorporating or excluding the three identified types of influence: intra-family, gender-age, and homophilic. This resulted in eight alternative models, designated as M1 through M8. The Akaike Information Criterion (AIC) was employed to identify the optimal model for each viewer. Consequently, each viewer was assigned to one of these eight models. The assignment of viewers to each model, both overall and within specific gender-age groups, is presented in Table 5.7.

Note) "x" indicates which type of influence was incorporated.

Overall, the majority of viewers (66%) were assigned to M2, which posits that only intra-family influence constitutes social influence. This suggests that intra-family influence is the most significant factor. The second-largest segment (13%) was assigned to M6, which takes into account both intra-family and homophilic influences. This suggests that the influence of other types of factors depends on the viewer.

A comparative analysis of different gender-age groups revealed several noteworthy observations:

1. Males aged 20–34 may be more likely to select programs independently of social influence than any other age group.
2. Males aged 35–49 may be more influenced by family than any other age group.
3. Children aged 4–12 may be more susceptible to intra-family and homophilic influences than any other age group.

Table 5.7 Proportion of optimal choice models across viewers (%)

	N	M1	M2	M3	M4	M5	M6	M7	M8
Inclusion of intra-family			x			x	x		x
Gender-age				x		x		x	x
Homophilic					x		x	x	x
Viewer: Total	1766	7.4	66.2	1.1	1.8	8.8	13.1	0.1	1.6
Aged 4–12	167	1.8	57.5	0.0	0.0	10.2	25.7	0.0	4.8
Aged 13–19	181	4.4	63.0	1.7	1.1	14.9	11.6	0.0	3.3
Male aged 20–34	220	15.5	63.2	3.2	3.2	8.6	5.5	0.0	0.9
Male aged 35–49	169	7.7	74.0	0.6	0.0	10.7	7.1	0.0	0.0
Male aged 50–	281	7.8	66.9	0.7	3.6	4.6	14.2	0.0	2.1
Female aged 20–34	207	7.7	70.5	1.9	0.0	8.7	10.6	0.0	0.5
Female aged 35–49	200	4.0	70.0	0.0	0.0	13.5	11.0	0.0	1.5
Female aged 50–	341	7.6	64.8	0.9	3.5	4.7	17.3	0.3	0.9

The results demonstrate the diversity of influence mechanisms, indicating that a comprehensive understanding of the specific influence dynamics across different demographics is crucial for the development of effective broadcasting and marketing strategies.

5.2.3 Goodness of Fit of the Simulated Outcomes

In the simulation, individual viewer choice models, calibrated separately as described above, are networked based on family affiliation, gender, age group, or neighborhood within the program space. The intra-family influence, which was treated in the calibration as having occurred simultaneously, is realized in the simulation through a non-cyclic path of influence in each family, which is generated at random. The gender-age and homophilic influences are determined by aggregating the values realized in the same time slot last week. While viewership would fluctuate according to the stochastic nature of individual viewers' program choices and social interactions, it could be stabilized by individual routinized viewing habits.Based on individual television viewing times, program broadcast schedules, and the position of these programs in the program space, we conducted 30 iterations of individual viewer choice simulations. These simulations utilized the calibrated and networked individual choice models, as previously discussed. Figure 5.5 illustrates the outcomes for a particular program (drama), with multiple dashed yellow lines denoting the simulated ratings and a single solid red line representing the observed rating. These results exhibit a general alignment, with the exception of a notable divergence in the program's final week. This discrepancy could be attributed to the inclusion of a special ending not accounted for in this model.

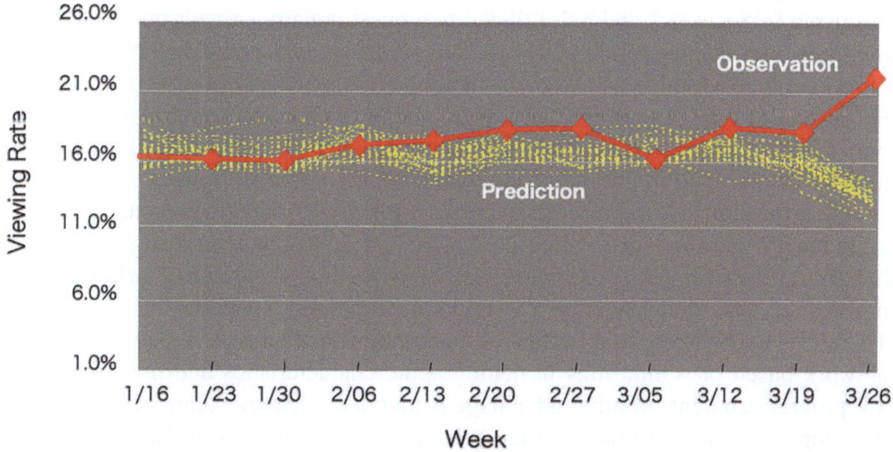

Fig. 5.5 Predicted and observed viewing rates for a program

Overall, across all programs, there was a moderate correlation between observed ratings and the averaged predictions, with a correlation coefficient of 0.699. While this is not a perfect correlation, it is noteworthy given the lack of program-specific content information fed into the simulation. This suggests that the model is generally effective in predicting TV viewing patterns based on individual preferences and social influence dynamics.

Additionally, this model offers a potential avenue for counterfactual simulations, which could provide insights into the impact of alterations in program positioning or broadcast schedules on viewership patterns. Moreover, it would be of interest to explore the potential impact of alterations to the influence relationships among viewers. To facilitate a more precise simulation, as previously stated, it would be beneficial to capture the program content at a granularity finer than the two-dimensional space employed in this study. Recent text analysis techniques may enable the dynamic measurement of program quality from program publicity, advertising, and even viewers' posts on social media. However, at the time of conducting this study, such an environment had not yet been established. Given that the study's primary objective was to understand social influences among viewers, these considerations remain as avenues for future exploration.

5.3 Summary and Discussion

A significant challenge in empirical agent-based modeling (EABM) is the availability of relevant data. The ideal scenario would involve longitudinal data that details individual behaviors, such as purchase records, combined with networks among individuals. However, obtaining such data can be challenging, except in unique situations, such as social media platforms with purchase functionalities (e.g., [62, 68]).

The diffusion study of the newly introduced mobile phone (iPhone), which is discussed in Sects. 5.1 and 5.2, utilized two questionnaire surveys conducted with the same respondents. A distinctive feature of this study was the dual measurement of new product adoption and word-of-mouth (WOM) networks among respondents. However, this type of survey is only applicable to a limited sample size and captures only a portion of the network that influences purchasing behavior. Furthermore, the number of observation points for individual behavior is also limited, thereby constraining the ability to capture the dynamic behavior of individual agents.

In the TV viewing survey described in Sect. 5.3, we obtained a large amount of behavioral data for each individual, sufficient to model individual behavior. The problem is that there is little information about the networks between them. Therefore, we compensated for this limitation by constructing a hypothetical social network based on similarities in demographic characteristics and preferences for TV program content. Another advantage is that because they belong to households in groups of several people, and the behavior of all members of the household is observed, it is possible to measure the propagation of influence through families. A comparison between the two aforementioned studies is presented in Table 5.8.

Table 5.8 Comparison of two EABMs

	iPhone diffusion in Japan	TV program viewing
Agent composition	Employees in a firm	TV viewers
Agent decision	Choice of whom to chat about a product and decision to adopt or consider it	Choice of a channel at each time slot given TV viewing
Rule change	Fixed	Fixed
Network	Empirically observed network	Virtually constructed based on the affiliation to intra-family, gender-age group, neighborhood in program space
Intervention	None	(Program position, air time)
Outcome	Diffusion rate, NPV	Viewing rates of programs

The estimation of parameters in an ABM, even when utilizing ideal data, presents a challenge that differs from the analysis typically conducted in statistics and econometrics. The conventional methodology entails formulating the goodness of fit to empirical data as a function and leveraging a nonlinear optimization algorithm. Grid search can be utilized when the number of parameters and their value range are limited. However, integrating statistical or machine learning techniques is advantageous for gaining insights into the reliability of the solution. As discussed in Sect. 5.2, regression trees may be a suitable approach for this purpose.

Gilbert [59] classifies ABM into three types: abstract models, middle-range models, and facsimile models. A typical abstract model is Schelling's segregation model [148], briefly introduced in Chap. 1, which does not take empirical validity based on real data into consideration at all. Rather, abstract models are oriented toward theoretical generality. Conversely, an emphasis on empirical validity often results in the development of facsimile models. A paradigmatic example of such a model is one that replicates the roads and traffic signals of an entire city in a computer for traffic simulation. The models examined in the initial four chapters of this book are abstract models. In contrast, the models introduced in this chapter are middle-range models that emphasize empirical validity in terms of inputs and outputs.

A variety of advanced methodologies are being employed to enhance the alignment of ABM with real data. Specifically, such methodological advancements are crucial for calibrating the parameters of facsimile models derived from large-scale data sets. One such approach is evolutionary computation methods, such as genetic algorithms, which facilitate the optimization of problems that are challenging to analyze (e.g., [25, 52, 151]). Recently, proposals have been made to employ Bayesian statistical methods (e.g., [27, 28, 103, 104, 135]). In recent years, there has been an uptick in research that has employed contemporary machine learning techniques, including neural networks and deep learning (e.g., [40, 152, 164]). It is anticipated that such research will continue to progress in the future.

It should be noted that the reliability of the calibrated parameter values for ABM is not guaranteed based on standard statistical theory. The procedures described in this chapter do not provide information regarding the significance of parameter estimates or their confidence intervals. One of the most significant challenges facing EABM is addressing this issue. One potential solution is to apply standard econometric methods to model agent behavior, as presented in Sect. 5.3. However, there are limitations and challenges associated with the direct application of existing econometric methods to ABM. Therefore, it is desirable to explore more advanced econometric methods and data analysis techniques from various fields to enhance the reliability and robustness of EABM studies.

Chapter 6
ABM with More Proactive Agents

In the ABM discussed in this book, agents (i.e., consumers) are primarily passive, merely forwarding information received from neighbors without modification. The network is considered static and not subject to active modification. However, if the agents are to proactively adapt to their environment, they can enhance their own payoffs by generating the information they should communicate to others and selecting the recipients to whom they should transmit the information. However, this extension introduces additional assumptions and increases the model's complexity, potentially compromising its empirical validity. In this chapter, we will present two studies conducted by the author that address cases where the agent exhibits greater adaptability and proactivity. One study examines the process by which influencers emerge from within the consumer population, while the other focuses on affiliate marketing, where influencers monetize their influence.

6.1 Emergence of Influence: Competition for Predictability

In Chaps. 2 and 3 of this book, we employed agent-based modeling (ABM) to examine the diffusion process of new products on social networks. In Chap. 4, we conducted a simulation of influencer marketing targeting hubs on networks. The analysis of empirical data indicates that the influence exerted by an individual cannot be solely attributed to their role as a hub. In light of the dynamic formation of networks, it is reasonable to assume that individuals with influence attract a considerable number of followers and that their influence increases in tandem with the growth of their network. This section introduces research utilizing agent-based modeling to address questions such as whether such processes occur by chance and

M. Mizuno, *Complex Modeling of Consumer Behavior*, Evolutionary Economics and Social Complexity Science 34,
https://doi.org/10.1007/978-4-431-54874-4_6

whether individuals with strong influence possess inherent characteristics that differentiate them from others.[1]

6.1.1 Modeling Individual Prediction on New Product Success

An influencer may be a celebrity, such as an entertainer or athlete, or an ordinary person. In this instance, we will examine the latter case, wherein the mechanism is more challenging to comprehend. Influencers can be celebrities, such as entertainers or athletes, or ordinary individuals. One hypothesis is that the capacity to anticipate trends before others is perceived as being "cool" [53], thereby generating that individual's influence. This ability is a factor in attracting a considerable number of followers on social media, among other things. In the case of products like fashion items, it is preferable to adopt trends before others, so if there are individuals who can accurately predict trends earlier, it is rational to follow them. We will now explore this scenario.

To model this kind of process, we may consider the following scenario: New products are introduced to the market at each time and are identified as $t = 1, \ldots, T$. Potential adopters (agents) $h = 1, \ldots, m$ estimate the success probability of a product introduced at time t, f_{ht}, just before its introduction into the market. This estimation is made based on the personal beliefs of the agents in question and the predictions made by their reference groups. For the purposes of this analysis, we define $\boldsymbol{F}_{ht}$ as agent h's reference group at t. The predictive performance of the reference group member, $j \in \boldsymbol{F}_{ht}$, is monitored and aggregated with a weight corresponding to the reliance score, which ranges from 0 to 1. The reliance score for agent h regarding agent j's prediction for product t is represented by q_{hjt}. As the agents' predictions are mutually dependent (Fig. 6.1), each agent's prediction is updated sequentially as follows:

$$f_{ht}(\tau) = r_h f_{ht}(t-1) + (1-r_h) \sum_{j \in \boldsymbol{F}_{ht}} q_{hjt} f_{ji}(\tau - 1) / \sum_{j \in \boldsymbol{F}_{ht}} q_{hj} \tag{6.1}$$

where parameter $r_h \in (0, 1)$ represents agent h's adherence, which is the degree to which agent h is inclined to adhere to their previous prediction and τ is the iteration step of the update. This mutual interaction is repeated until the value of $f_{ht}(\tau)$ reaches a certain steady-state level. The initial values $f_{ht}(0)$ are generated at random, with a uniform distribution over the interval (0, 1). Should the estimated probability of success for a given product exceed a specified threshold, the agent will adopt it.

[1] This section revises the work of Mizuno et al. [114], incorporating new figures.

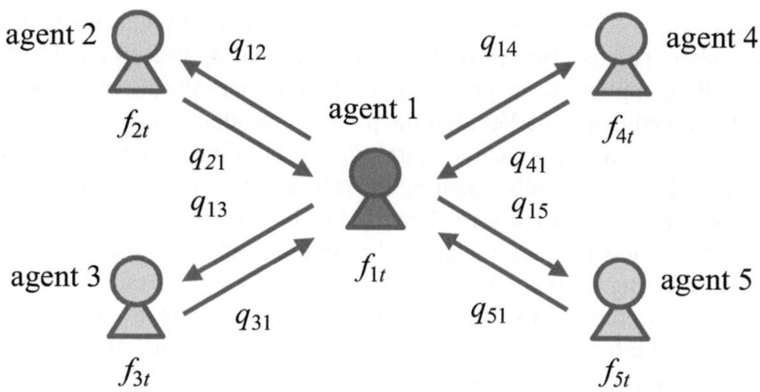

Fig. 6.1 Prediction process based on reliance to members of a reference group

6.1.2 *Modeling Network Reconstruction for Accurate Prediction*

The agents are initially situated within a two-dimensional square lattice space, with the margins looped (in accordance with the periodic boundary condition). In accordance with the Moore neighborhood concept, it is assumed that each agent has eight direct neighbors. To facilitate interaction with a broader range of indirect neighbors, each agent is assumed to have a specific field of view, defined as the set of agents situated at a designated distance, ϕ, from agent h. As its membership is dynamic, contingent on the influx of new product introductions, a field of view is denoted by $\boldsymbol{V}_{ht}$. In the initial period ($t = 1$), a reference group is equal to a field of view ($\boldsymbol{F}_{h1} = \boldsymbol{V}_{h1}$).

In our model, the reliance score on members or former members of the reference group is heterogeneous and time-varying. Consequently, the relationships between agents can be expressed as a weighted temporal directed network. The degree of reliance is updated based on the accuracy of each agent's prediction regarding the success of a new product. In other words, the reliance increases for agents whose predictions are accurate, while it decreases for agents whose predictions are inaccurate. Specifically, the reliance that agent h has on agent $j \in \boldsymbol{F}_{hi}$ is updated in accordance with the following procedure when a new product, designated as $t + 1$, is introduced:

$$q_{hj,t+1} = (1-\gamma)q_{hjt} + \gamma, \text{if the prediction made by } j \text{ at } t \text{ is accurate} \tag{6.2}$$

$$q_{hj,t+1} = (1-\gamma)q_{hjt}, \text{otherwise}$$

where parameter $\gamma \in (0, 1)$ represents the speed of updating reliance on a reference group member. This is also referred to as the internal update speed. The updated reliance will be applied to the prediction of the product introduced at $t + 1$, which will be introduced in the market after the product introduced at t.

As a more dynamic approach to learning, it is possible to reconstruct the reference group rather than merely updating the reliance placed on each member of the reference group. One method for achieving this is to remove members whose reliance has fallen below the individualized threshold ($q_{h0} \in (0, 1)$) from their reference group. If monitoring the predictions of others necessitates a certain degree of effort, it is reasonable to replace them with more reliable members, even if their predictions are already infrequently reflected in their own predictions. The reconstruction process of a reference group is outlined in Fig. 6.2.

For agents that have been excluded from the reference group, their prediction performance will no longer be subject to direct monitoring. Nevertheless, should the predictive performance of these agents, who are within the same field of view, subsequently improve, it is probable that they will be re-included within the reference group after indirectly becoming aware of their reputation. In this model, we posit that an agent's reputation is shaped by the degree of reliance that other agents in their reference group place on the excluded agent. However, in the event that there are only a few members monitoring the agent in question (i.e., if most members exclude the agent), the degree of reliance must be estimated as low. Accordingly, the presumed reputation of an unmonitored agent should be established at a level that is considerably below the threshold of reliance (i.e., at half the threshold). Therefore, we propose the following formula for agent h to calculate the reputation indicator for agent k, who has been excluded from h's reference group ($k \notin \boldsymbol{F}_{ht}$):

$$\tilde{q}_{hkt} = \sum_{j \in \boldsymbol{V}_{ht}} \left(a_{hj} a_{jk} q_{jkt} + \left(1 - a_{hj}\right) a_{jk} q_{h0} / 2 \right) / \left|\boldsymbol{V}_{ht}\right| \tag{6.3}$$

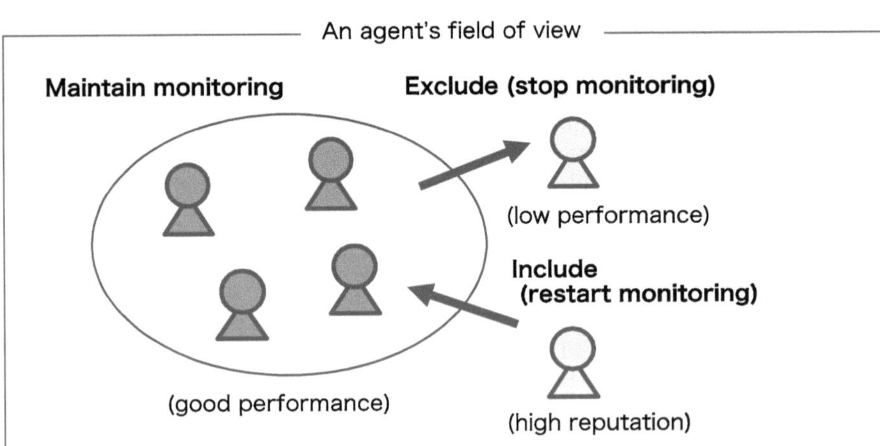

Fig. 6.2 Reconstruction of each agent's reference group based on reliance or reputation

where a_{hj} is a binary variable that assumes the value of 1 when agent h includes agent j in h's reference group and 0 otherwise, and $|\boldsymbol{V}_{ht}|$ indicates the number of agents who are within agent h's field of view. The reputation index calculated in the aforementioned manner, is used to update the reliance of agent $k \notin \boldsymbol{F}_{ht}$ as follows:

$$q_{hk,t+1} = (1-\nu) q_{hkt} + \nu \cdot \tilde{q}_{hkt} \tag{6.4}$$

where $\nu \in (0, 1)$ represents the speed of updating the reliance on former member of the reference group (or external updating speed). Should the value of $q_{hk,t+1}$ exceed the threshold q_{h0}, agent h will re-include agent k within the reference group.

The values of the parameters γ (reliance-updating speed for members of reference groups) and ν (reliance-updating speed for former members of reference groups) are identical for all agents in each run, constituting simulation conditions. The combination of the levels of γ and ν generates the following four types of markets:

- If both γ and ν are elevated, the low-predictive members are expeditiously excluded from the reference group, while high-predictive former members are re-included with greater alacrity. In general, the reconstruction of reference groups occurs at a faster rate.
- If γ is higher but ν is lower, exclusion happens faster, but re-inclusion takes longer. In this scenario, agents may tend to "purify" their reference groups.
- If γ is lower but ν is higher, the exclusion process takes place at a slower rate, while the re-inclusion process is relatively rapid. It can be argued that agents demonstrate a certain degree of tolerance towards both those within and outside of each reference group.
- If both γ and ν are lower, the reconstruction of the reference groups takes longer.

6.1.3 Networks Generated by Inter-agent Interaction

A simulation of the aforementioned model is conducted with 100 agents, representing potential adopters. The following rules uniformly apply to all agents and all runs:

- Each agent performs 15 iterations of the subjective probability update for product success (f_{ht}),
- If the probability exceeds 0.5, the agent will adopt the product,
- A diffusion rate exceeding 0.5 is indicative of a successful outcome.
- New products are introduced in a sequential manner on 100 times.

The conditions varying across runs are:

- The internal update speed: $\gamma \in \{0.2, 0.4, 0.6, 0.8\}$,
- The external update speed: $\nu \in \{0.0, 0.2, 0.4, 0.6, 0.8\}$,
- The distance in a field of view: $\phi \in \{1, 2\}$.

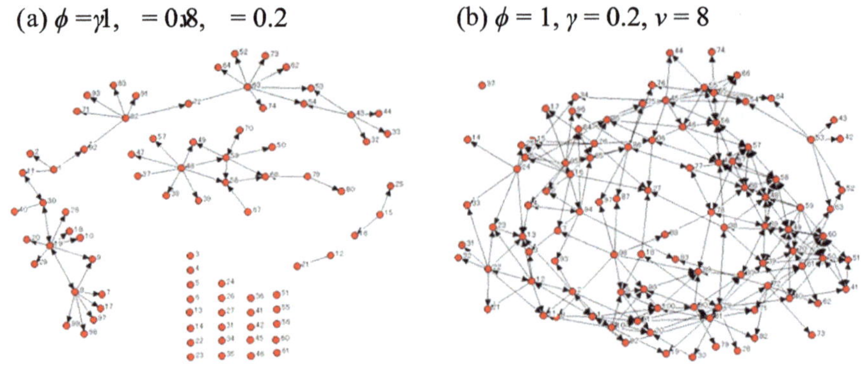

Fig. 6.3 Examples of networks among agents generated by simulation

The formation of reference groups results in the construction of a directed network, with an arrow drawn from agent h to k if and only if h has included k within h's reference group. The sample networks that emerged under (1) $\phi = 1$, $\gamma = 0.8$, and $\nu = 0.2$ and of (2) $\phi = 1$, $\gamma = 0.2$, and $\nu = 0.8$ in the steady-states are illustrated in Fig. 6.3. In the case of (1), the speed of exclusion from the reference group is high, and the speed of re-inclusion once excluded is slow. This results in a strong tendency to purify the reference group, and the network that is ultimately generated is sparse. In contrast, in the case of (2), the opposite is true, and the network is dense. This is due to the tolerance towards both internal and external members of the reference group.

In order to ascertain the impact of the simulation conditions, five runs were conducted for each combination of alternative values of ϕ, γ, and ν. In each run, the values of r_h and q_{h0} are generated as uniform random numbers within the interval (0, 1), and vary among agents. The mean value of reliance across all agents reached a steady-state in every run through the repetition of new product introductions, which stabilized the networks among agents. In the final network, the indegree of each agent represents the number of other individuals included within the agent's reference group, signifying the number of followers in the network among agents. In contrast, the outdegree of each agent represents the number of other individuals that the agent has incorporated into their own reference group, thereby indicating the number of individuals they follow.

The properties of the resulting networks are summarized in the indegree and outdegree distributions. The indegree distributions when the field of view is minimal ($\phi = 1$) are shown in Fig. 6.4. For most combinations of γ and ν, the majority of agents have an indegree of 0, and the number of agents decreases as the indegree increases. When all agents have a strong tendency to purify the reference group (represented by a large γ and a small ν in the lower left of the figure), the number of agents with an indegree of 0 increases.

As shown in Fig. 6.5, the outdegree distribution remains consistent when the same combination of parameters is maintained, indicating that the resulting

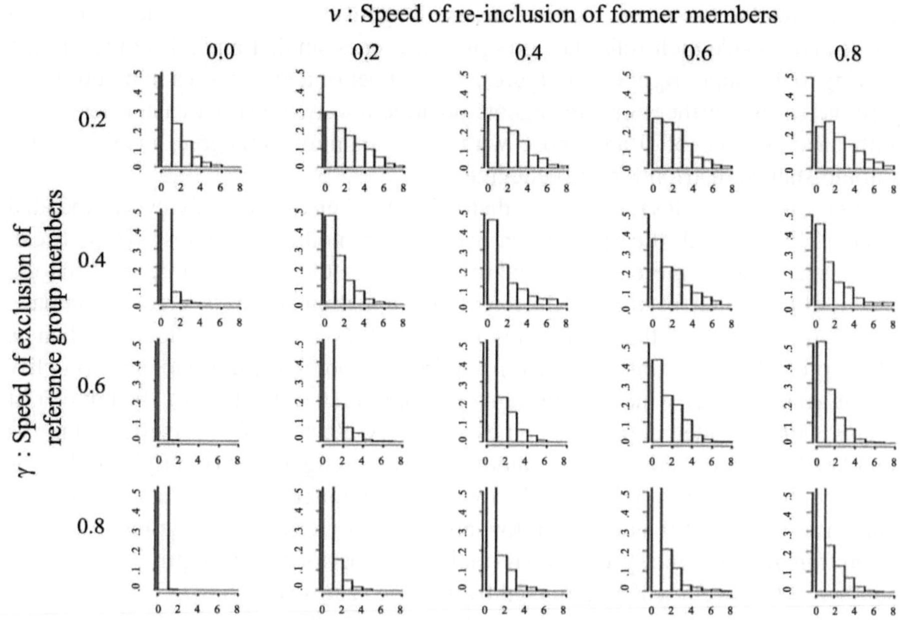

Fig. 6.4 Indegree distributions of networks generated when $\phi = 1$

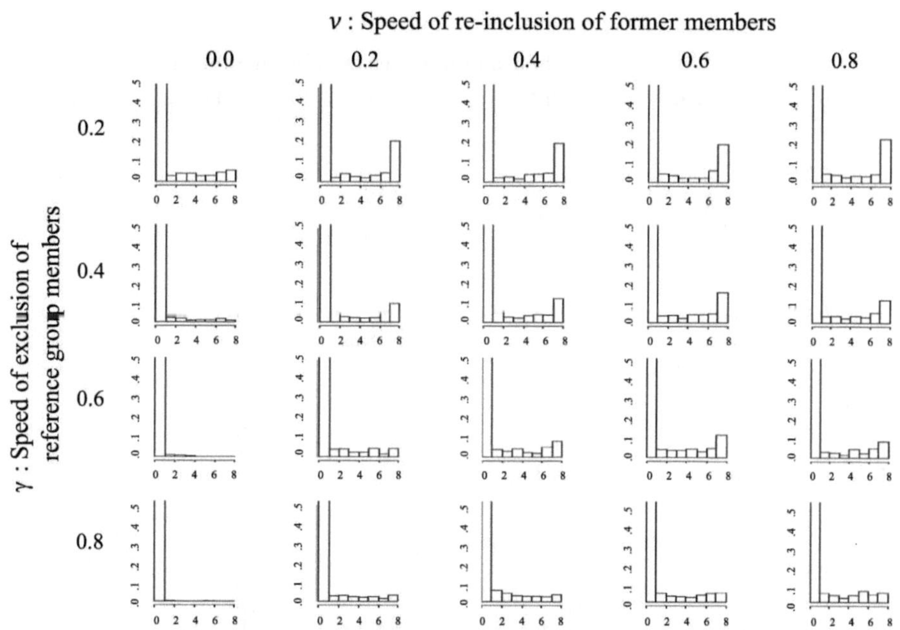

Fig. 6.5 Outdegree distributions of networks generated when $\phi = 1$

networks tend to be sparse. Conversely, as all agents become more tolerant of both inside and outside their reference groups (γ becomes smaller and ν becomes larger, moving to the upper right of the figure), the number of agents with a non-zero indegree increases. Furthermore, the agents polarize into two distinct categories: those with an outdegree of 0 and those with the maximum outdegree, resulting in a bathtub-shaped distribution of outdegrees.

Figure 6.4 illustrates the indegree distributions when the field of view is expanded as $\phi = 2$. In general, the distribution becomes unimodal and almost symmetrical, and this tendency is more pronounced in cases where the overall γ (internal updating speed) of the agents is small or the ν (external updating speed) is large. A comparison of the effects of these variables indicates that γ is more influential than ν. Therefore, when γ is substantial and ν is minimal, indicating a pronounced proclivity for agents to purify the reference group (bottom left of the figure), the number of agents with an indegree of 0 becomes markedly elevated. Conversely, when γ is small and ν is large, indicating greater tolerance among agents (top right of the figure), the distribution of indegrees is not simply symmetrical. In a social culture of tolerance, in which all agents with low predictive performance are gradually eliminated from the reference group and re-inclusion is performed promptly, a significant number of followers will be attracted by average agents (Fig. 6.6).

As the field of view (ϕ) increases from 1 to 2, the distribution of outdegree retains a bathtub-shaped nature (Fig. 6.7). In the region where γ is 0.4 or less and ν is 0.2 or more, the outdegree is distributed more symmetrically, indicating a clear

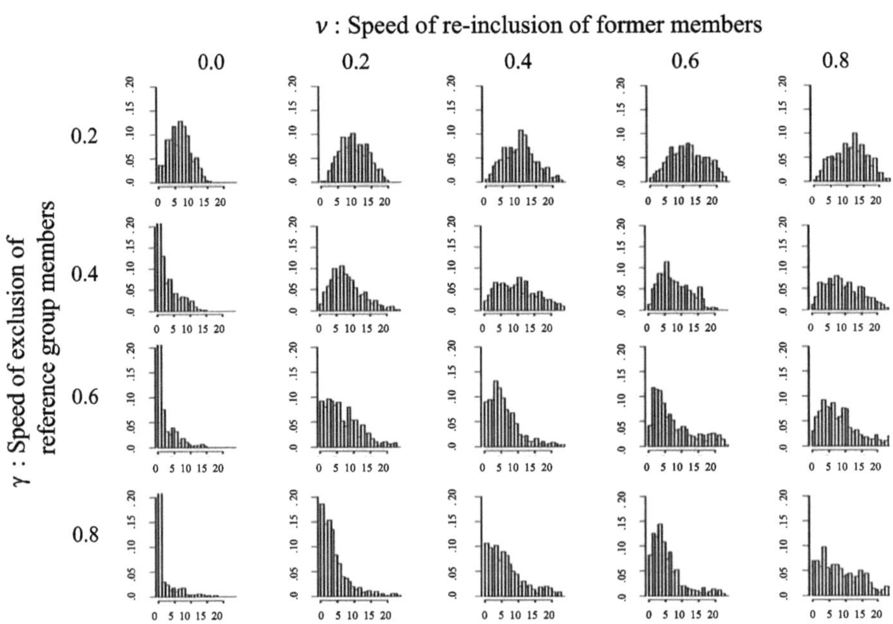

Fig. 6.6 Indegree distributions of networks generated when $\phi = 2$

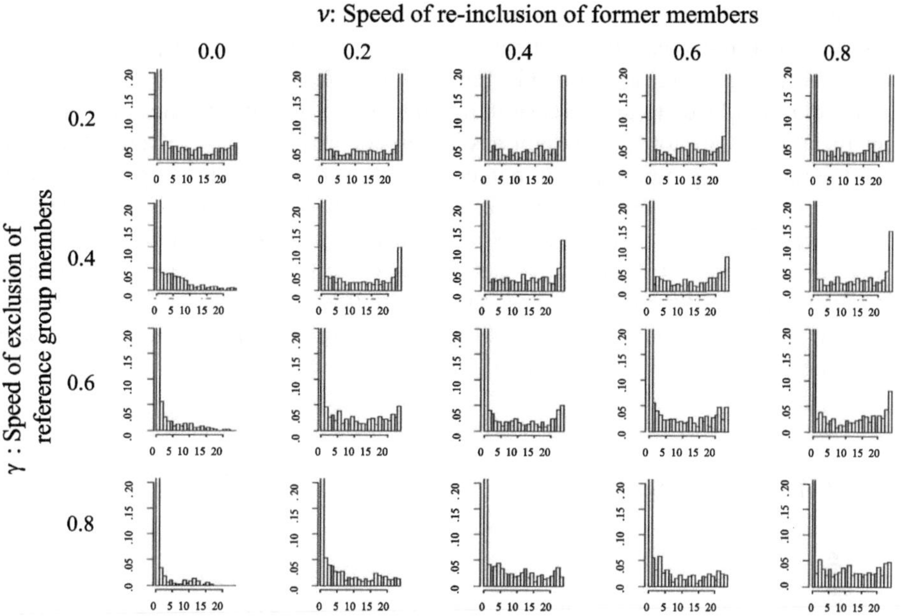

Fig. 6.7 Outdegree distributions of networks generated when $\phi = 2$

polarization into two extremes: either almost no one is followed, or the maximum number of agents within the field of view is followed. This is in contrast to the observation that the indegree distributions in the same area are symmetrical and unimodal.

6.1.4 Emergence of Influencer-Follower Structure

In the preceding section, we investigated the impact of key factors inherent to all agents (social culture), specifically the two types of speeds in reference group updating and the size of the field of view. The objective was to ascertain the influence of these factors on the properties of emergent networks. In this section, we analyze the diversity of individual positions within the generated networks. The distinguishing factor between agents in this model is the degree of adherence to their initial prediction (r_h) when updating their assessment of the probability of success for a new product (Eq. 6.1), as well as the threshold of reliance (q_{h0}) when incorporating the remaining agents in the reference group, which are distributed uniformly between 0 and 1. If we consider these as individual characteristics of agents, we will investigate which characteristics increase the indegree of the network; in other words, lead an agent to have more followers. It is generally assumed that having a large number of followers fulfills the conditions of an influencer.

Figure 6.8 illustrates the correlation between the characteristics of agents (r_h, q_{h0}) and the mean indegree for each field of view size (ϕ). First, when $\phi = 1$, it can be observed that a decrease in the adherence to prior prediction (r_h) and the reliance threshold (q_{h0}) leads to an increase in the indegree of the agent. This suggests that an agent who does not stick to their past prediction and has a low reliance threshold for the reference group will gain numerous followers and occupy a position as an influencer. In other words, the greater one's receptivity to alternative predictions, the more likely it is that one's prediction will be accepted by one's neighbors, thereby enhancing their predictive performance. This suggests that being open to other opinions and being flexible in one's predictions may be an effective strategy for becoming an influencer. The possible mechanism behind this phenomenon will be discussed in the following section.

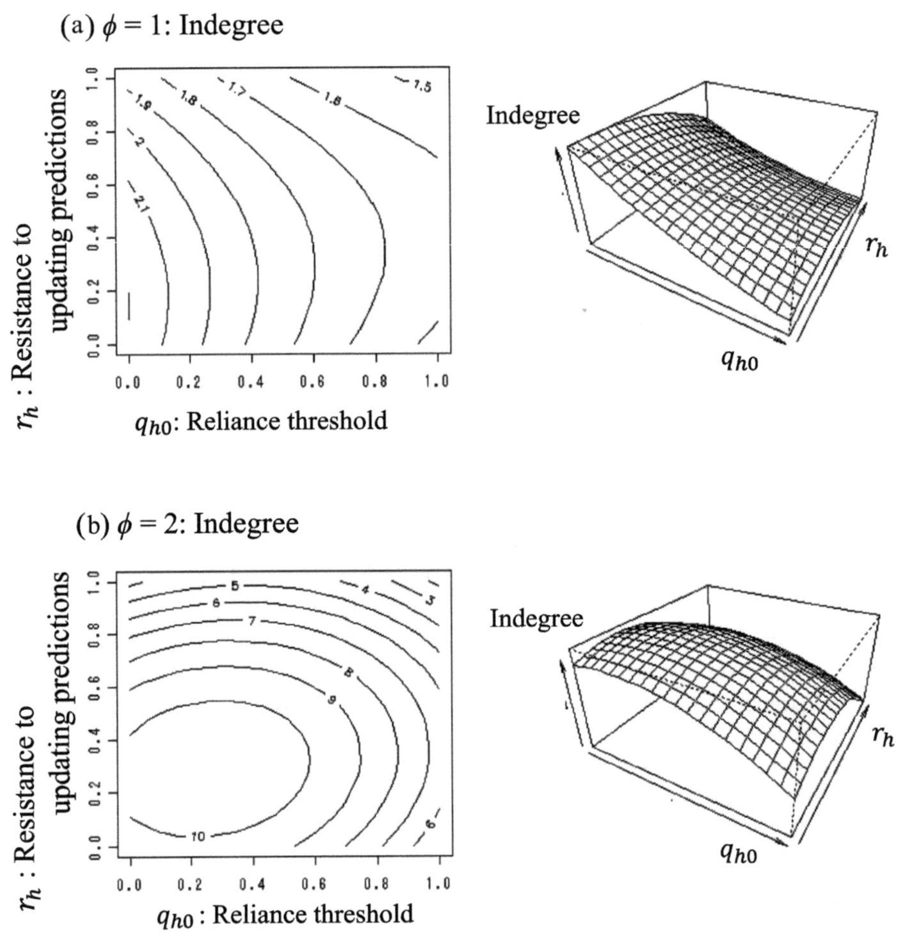

Fig. 6.8 The relationship between each agent's traits and indegree

However, when a broader field of view is considered, the situation changes slightly. The maximum value of indegree is observed when r_h and q_{h0} are low, but not at their minimum levels. In other words, when one's field of view is wide, it is preferable to maintain a certain degree of adherence to one's own predictions and to incorporate some level of reconstruction of one's reference group in order to increase the number of followers.[2]

The following section will examine the relationship between individual characteristics and the mean indegree. As illustrated in Fig. 6.9, a reduction in the threshold for reliance (q_{h0}) is associated with an increase in outdegree. This finding suggests that agents attempt to monitor a greater number of individuals within their field of view, thereby expanding their reference group. It follows logically that a lower threshold for reliance on members of the reference group results in a larger reference group. Notably, this relationship holds even when the field of view is further expanded.

As previously stated, the agent with the greatest number of followers, or the agent with the highest indegree, can be regarded as an influencer. When the agent possesses an extensive field of view ($\phi = 2$), it becomes evident that there is a variation in influencers' outdegree, or the size of their reference groups. At one end of the spectrum, the outdegree reaches its maximum level, and the reference group covers the entire field of view. It is hypothesized that they enhance their predictive performance by collecting a diverse array of information because the threshold for reliance on reference group members is low. At the opposite end of the spectrum, the scope of the reference group is slightly smaller than its maximum, as the reliance threshold is low but not minimal. In this case, the high predictive performance is due to the careful monitoring of selected agents. These results suggest that two distinct strategies could enhance the precision of predicting the success of new products.

The agent with the smallest indegree in Fig. 6.8 is also the agent with the smallest outdegree in Fig. 6.9. The agent with the fewest followers and the most limited reference group is thus isolated from the network. When the field of view is at its narrowest ($\phi = 1$), an agent that is reluctant to alter its own predictions and has a high reliance threshold becomes isolated. However, when the field of view is expanded ($\phi - 2$), even if the agent does not adhere to its own predictions at all, if the reliance threshold is high, the agent becomes isolated. In other words, the reliance threshold is more critical for network formation (i.e., the construction of a reference group). An isolated agent does not trust the predictions of others at all, and its predictive ability decreases, so it ceases to be monitored by others.

The number of indegrees is relatively low, but the outdegrees of agents with a moderate size can be considered typical followers. These agents are highly adherent

[2]While the results are not presented here, even in the case of simulations with an expanded field of view, the relationship between individual characteristics and the mean indegree is essentially similar to what is observed in the case of $\phi = 2$.

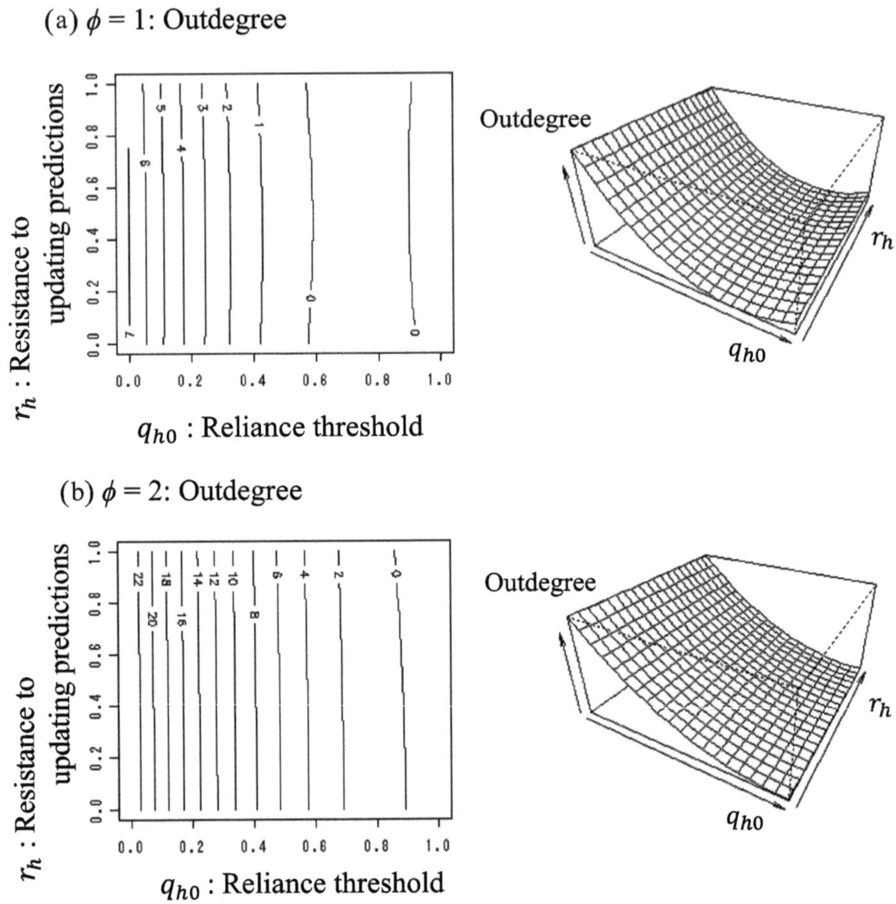

Fig. 6.9 The relationship between each agent's traits and outdegree

to their own predictions, which limits their ability to improve their forecasting accuracy and attract even a small number of followers. However, the reliance threshold is moderate, allowing them to follow numerous agents, resulting in a moderately sized reference group. Those who aspire to be the first to predict trends and gain influence over others should consider weakening their adherence to their own predictions and lowering their reliance threshold, as influencers do. The potential to adjust the parameters that we have defined as individual characteristics so that each agent can increase its own influence represents an intriguing avenue for future expansion of the model.

6.1.5 Competition for Predictability as a Source of Social Influence

The models introduced in this section examine the processes by which potential adopters differentiate between influencers and followers in a context where new products are introduced sequentially. The assumption is that agents make decisions to predict the success of a new product and, if they predict it to be successful, they will adopt it. This can be seen as a "backing the winner" strategy. The adoption of new products with high diffusion rates by potential adopters has been regarded as imitation within the Bass model and GLM model. In this model, there is no difference in the timing of adoption by agents, as all predictions are made simultaneously to determine whether or not to adopt. The reasoning that the likelihood of others adopting is a signal of quality is inappropriate in this model as there is no information about true quality. The only information that agents rely on to adopt new products is the predicted diffusion rate.

This model addresses the phenomenon of self-fulfilling predictions in the context of product adoption. Each agent's decision to adopt or not adopt a new product is based on its own predictive evaluation. If a majority of agents predict the product's success and adopt it, their prediction becomes self-fulfilling. A similar outcome occurs when the majority predicts failure. If agents make random predictions, a majority formed by chance is capable of making accurate predictions. If this process is repeated, the agent who earns the trust of its followers will attract additional followers and become an influencer.

The reason why not all agents can become influencers is that there are individual differences in the extent to which they adhere to their own predictions or follow those of others. Agents who tend to follow the predictions of others are more likely to adopt the majority's predictions regarding the success or failure of new products and are therefore more likely to align with the winning choice. As a result, they tend to gain many followers.

Another factor to consider is the individual differences in tolerance, or reliance threshold, for the members of the reference group. While it may appear logical to exclude agents that consistently fail in their predictions from the reference group and not use them as a reference for one's own predictions, this approach may not be optimal. The predictions themselves are not based on objective criteria, such as the true quality of the new product, and thus are susceptible to random influences. It is therefore more rational to monitor as many agents as possible and average their predictions. However, if one has a broad field of view, it is preferable to adhere to one's own predictions while selectively choosing reference group members, as this will contribute to maximizing the number of followers.

This phenomenon is frequently observed in the context of convenience goods, where the intrinsic quality may remain opaque even after initial adoption. In the case of goods such as fashion and entertainment, many consumers may be more concerned with whether or not they adopt new products to appear ahead of trends by adopting them than with the true quality of the goods themselves. In other words, it is not considered "cool" to adopt new products after they have become popular. Instead, it is preferable to be able to anticipate the success of a new product immediately upon its introduction. This is exactly what can be defined as a trendsetter.

There is research that claims the reviews of film critics (who could be considered a type of influencer) do not affect audience turnout, but rather align with the preferences of the majority audience [50]. If this is correct, it suggests that film critics predict whether a film will be a hit or not, whether they are aware of it or not. Our model presented earlier suggests that the phenomenon of influencers influencing the majority may be generated without objective evidence through social interactions between agents.

Some may argue that attributing the success of a new product solely to chance is an overly simplistic perspective. The notion that, while interaction with others is crucial, the intrinsic quality of a product also exerts a significant influence is substantiated by a seminal experiment on music downloads [146]. The experiment demonstrated that the number of downloads by others had a pronounced impact on the choices made by the subjects, yet their original preferences also exerted a certain influence. From this perspective, it would be highly meaningful to extend the proposed model.

6.2 Monetization of Influence: Affiliate Marketing

Affiliate marketing represents a system through which influencers can monetize their influence. Affiliates utilize their own websites, typically blogs, to display advertisements for products from third-party companies. In the event that users who visit the website click on the advertisement and subsequently make a purchase, the affiliate receives a reward from the company or the affiliate marketing service operator. In some instances, the influencer is responsible for selecting the advertisement to be inserted, while in other instances, the operator of the affiliate marketing service is tasked with inserting the advertisements that match the influencer's website content. In the former case, the influencer is the decision-maker of which products are advertised and when. Consequently, the advertiser is unable to control the insertion of advertisements unilaterally, as is customary with traditional media advertising. The extent to which this novel form of advertising will evolve in the future is contingent upon the interplay between the influencers who furnish the content and become affiliates, the general users who consume the content and respond to the advertising, and the advertiser companies and operators. To elucidate these intricate phenomena, we will present an illustrative example of research that employs an agent-based model.[3]

---

[3] This section provides a summary of the findings from Mizuno [111], with additional discussion.

6.2.1 Affiliate Marketing as an Empowerment

The capacity of users to spread information on social media platforms such as Twitter (now X), Facebook, YouTube, Instagram, and TikTok illustrates a shift in power from traditional mass media to individual users. Affiliate marketing represents an effort to leverage this empowerment as a communication channel for businesses. Affiliates retain the autonomy to determine whether or not to insert advertisements into their websites, such as blogs, a decision that is not entirely within the control of companies. If mass marketing is defined as one-to-many communication, then social media marketing can be conceptualized as a platform for many-to-many communication [78].

In affiliate marketing, the distance between the consumer and the advertisement may be shorter than in mass marketing (Fig. 6.10). This is due to the fact that the website provides content that is more closely aligned with the consumer's interests, which naturally leads to the formation of a strong sense of intimacy. To illustrate, an advertisement for a new mystery novel posted on a blog dedicated to mystery novels will likely be clicked on more frequently than on other websites. The capacity to target audiences with precision is a key strength of affiliate marketing. However, the number of individuals with an interest in specific topics is often limited, resulting in a narrower reach for advertising compared to mass media. Consequently, affiliate marketing serves as a valuable complement to mass marketing rather than a substitute.

As previously stated, it is challenging for companies to maintain comprehensive control over affiliate marketing. Consequently, research on affiliate marketing has focused on key areas such as how to select affiliates [127] and how to motivate affiliates through monetary incentives [101, 129]. This research, however, focuses on a more macro-level issue and aims to identify the conditions under which the affiliate marketing market expands. To achieve this, we will employ ABM, which conceptualizes social phenomena as the interaction of multiple agents. In this approach, we will establish two categories of agents: influencers, who determine which advertisements to insert into their websites, and followers, who decide whether or not to engage with advertisements on the websites they frequently visit. While advertisers and operators would typically be significant agents, for the sake of simplicity, we will exclude them from consideration in this study.

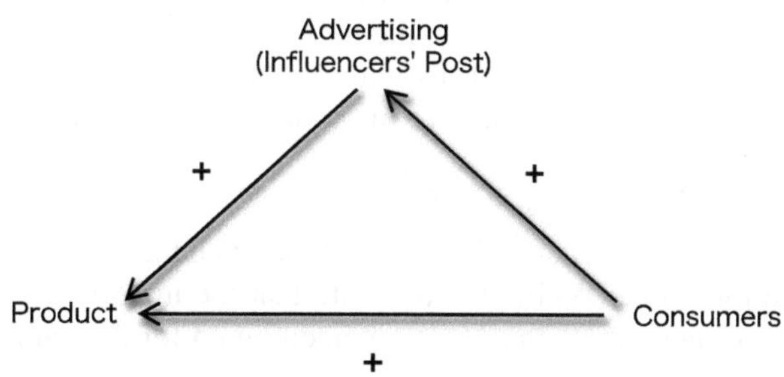

Fig. 6.10 Triad balance explaining the effectiveness of advertising

6.2.2 Modeling Affiliate Influencer Behavior

We consider influencers who have adopted affiliate marketing and model their decision-making process for selecting which advertisements to insert on their websites. In each period, the decision regarding which advertisement to post on the website of influencer i, where $i = 1, \ldots, I$, for product p, where $p = 1, 2, \ldots, P$, is made (i.e., the advertisement mix decision). It is assumed that multiple products can be advertised simultaneously. If a_{ipt} is a binary variable that takes the value of 1 if influencer i posts an advertisement for product p on their website in time t, and 0 otherwise, the action of influencer i can be expressed by the following vector:

$$\boldsymbol{a}_{it} = \left(a_{i1t}, \ldots, a_{ipt}, \ldots, a_{iPt}\right) \tag{6.5}$$

For the purposes of this analysis, it is assumed that the topics of the content posted by influencer i are fixed as the following vector:

$$\boldsymbol{b}_{i} = \left(b_{i1}, \ldots, b_{ik}, \ldots, b_{iK}\right) \tag{6.6}$$

where the value of b_{ik} is equal to 1 if influencer i is posting about topic k (where $k = 1, 2, \ldots, K$), and 0 otherwise. In addition, it is assumed that a single influencer is capable of handling multiple topics. The assumption that the topics posted by influencers remain static is justified by the thought that, in the nascent stages of social media, influencers were primarily driven by a desire to disseminate their personal beliefs and interests, rather than by the prospect of financial reward. This assumption will be challenged in the study presented in Sect. 6.3.

Influencers have the option of modifying their advertising mix on a quarterly basis. In accordance with the hypothesis proposed by Nelson and Winter [123], when affiliate revenue declines, we will assume that they either randomly alter their advertising mix (through mutation) or imitate the strategies employed by those who have achieved success. Based on the strategy to update their advertising mix in the event of a decline in revenue relative to the previous time period, we will categorize influencers into two distinct groups:

1. Random walkers: They randomly select one of the advertisements inserted on the website and cease inserting it, and then randomly select one of the other product categories and insert an advertisement for that in its place.
2. Imitator: They choose the influencer with the highest revenue from the previous time period who deals with the most similar topics, and copy their advertising mix. The similarity in topics between influencers i and j is calculated by $1 - \sum_{k=1}^{K} \left| b_{ik} - b_{jk} \right|$.

The notion that an imitator could ascertain the revenue of other affiliates may appear implausible. While it is accurate that the majority of influencers refrain from disclosing their revenue, it is not uncommon for the number of visitors to a website to be displayed or for rankings to be introduced on third-party websites. This suggests that it may be possible to estimate which influencers generate the highest revenue to some extent.

6.2.3 Modeling Follower Behavior

Subsequently, we examine the agents designated as $h = 1, \ldots, H$, who are respectively assigned as followers to the given set of influencers. For simplicity, we assume that the specific influencers they follow remain constant. This relationship is expressed in a bipartite network of influencers and followers, as previously outlined in Sect. 4.3. It should be noted that there is no following relationship among influencers, among followers, or from influencers to followers. In the study discussed in Sect. 6.2, we analyze the differences in results due to differences in the network, excluding the possibility that the network changes dynamically.

The likelihood of a follower purchasing a product advertised on an influencer's website is contingent upon their preference for the product in question. Let v_{hp} be a variable that assumes the value of 1 if follower h has a preference for the advertisement for product p, and 0 otherwise. The following vector is then defined:

$$\boldsymbol{v}_h = \left(v_{h1}, \ldots, v_{hp}, \ldots, v_{hP}\right) \tag{6.7}$$

As previously stated, it is assumed that this vector will remain constant over time.

Upon visiting an influencer's website, a follower will consider purchasing a product that matches their preferences (as defined in Eq. (6.9)) if it is advertised (as defined in Eq. 6.5). In the event that there is only one candidate product, the follower will proceed with the purchase of that item. Conversely, in the event that there are multiple candidates, the follower will randomly choose one of the candidates and proceed with the purchase. When a follower purchases a product through an affiliate marketing advertisement, the influencer is paid a certain amount of affiliate commission. Assuming that there is no difference in marginal revenue, the affiliate revenue earned by the influencer will be proportional to the number of followers who purchase from that website.

As a criterion for deciding which influencer's website to follow, we consider the congruence between the follower's topic preferences and the topics offered by the influencer. We consider a binary variable u_{hk} that takes the value 1 if the follower h prefers the content of topic k, and 0 otherwise, and define the following topic preference vector:

$$\boldsymbol{u}_h = \left(u_{h1}, \ldots, u_{hk}, \ldots, u_{hK}\right) \tag{6.8}$$

The topic congruence of this vector and the content provided by the influencer is calculated as follows:

$$TC(i,h) = 1 - \sum_{k=1}^{K} |b_{ik} - u_{hk}| / K \tag{6.9}$$

If a follower can identify the websites that best match his or her topic preferences, it would be reasonable to assume that they would follow influencers that maximize this criterion. However, here we consider another possibility: the case where followers follow so as to maximize the congruence between their product preferences and the ad mix (hereafter we refer to this simply as "ad congruence"). Ad congruence is calculated as follows:

$$AC(i,h) = 1 - \sum_{p=1}^{P} |a_{ip} - v_{hp}| / K \tag{6.10}$$

The assumption that followers choose the websites they visit to view advertisements may seem unnatural at first, but considering the scenario in which the most desirable network for both advertisers and affiliates is achieved serves as a benchmark for evaluating the simulation results.

Since data on the bipartite network between influencers and followers are not available, it has been artificially generated. The procedure is to prioritize linking to pairs with high tie(i, h):

$$tie(i,h) = \omega_1 \cdot RN + \omega_2 \cdot TC(i,h) + \omega_3 \cdot AC(i,h) \tag{6.11}$$

where *RN* is a uniformly distributed random number in the interval (0, 1), and the weights ω_1, ω_2, ω_3 are non-negative values that add up to 1. Constraints based on real data are imposed on the indegree indegree (i.e., the number of followers an influencer has) of influencer nodes and the outdegree (i.e., the number of websites a follower visits) of follower nodes.

By changing the values of each component of $\boldsymbol{\omega} = (\omega_1, \omega_2, \omega_3)$, different types of networks can be generated. If $\boldsymbol{\omega} = (1, 0, 0)$, it becomes a random graph, if $\boldsymbol{\omega} = (0, 1, 0)$, it becomes a perfect topic-congruent network, and if $\boldsymbol{\omega} = (0, 0, 1)$, it becomes a perfect ad-congruent network.

6.2.4 Simulation Partially Using Empirical Data

In this study, the attributes of each agent are assigned based on data obtained from online questionnaire surveys conducted among Internet users, with the exception of information pertaining to the network between influencers and followers. The first survey was conducted in December 2011 for a sample of 361 affiliate bloggers who had been posting at least once a month and had participated in affiliate marketing programs. The collected data provide information on the attributes of affiliate bloggers. The second survey was conducted at around the same time for 412 target followers, who had visited a blog at least once in the past month and had purchased a product advertised there at least once in the past 6 months, providing information on the attributes of the possible targets of affiliate marketing. Both samples were extracted from a survey company panel comprising web users aged 13 and over. The information obtained from them is outlined in Table 6.1.

Affiliate influencers correspond to influencers in the above model, while target blog visitors correspond to followers in the model.[4] In order to preserve the heterogeneity of users, the information provided by each respondent is transferred to an agent within the model, rather than aggregating their responses. However, if the respondents are assigned to the agents on a one-to-one basis, the number of agents in the model would be limited by the sample size of the survey data. Therefore, a certain number of respondents from each survey are randomly selected through resampling with replacement and individually assigned to an agent in the model. This approach is analogous to the bootstrap method [49]. Therefore, in principle, it may be feasible to apply this method to infer confidence intervals for ABM results.

Influencers (bloggers) can be classified into two categories: random walkers and imitators. This distinction is based on the differing strategies employed by each group in modifying the advertising mix. If we assume that $\lambda \times 100\%$ of influencers are random walkers, then λ is set to five levels: with possible values of 0.1, 0.3, 0.5, 0.7, and 0.9. The weights for the network generation criteria ($\boldsymbol{w} = (w_1, w_2, w_3)$) are set to seven combinations, as illustrated in Table 6.2. In other words, when the network is formed based on any one of the criteria alone (Options 1, 3, 7), when two criteria are considered equally (Options 2, 4, 6), and when it is formed by equally considering three criteria (Option 5), the resulting network will have the indicated weighting.

The following is the procedure for conducting the simulation of the above model:

1. Generation of Agents: 100 individuals are randomly selected from the responses to an online-survey of affiliate bloggers ($N = 361$) and their attributes are assigned to each of influencer agents. Additionally, 1000 individuals are randomly selected from the sample of target blog visitors ($N = 412$) and their attributes are

Table 6.1 Overview of surveys as an empirical foundation for the model

User type	Items in survey	Values	Variable in the model
Affiliate bloggers	Content topics (29)	{0, 1}	$(b_{i1t}, \ldots, b_{ikt}, \ldots, b_{iKt})$
	Products advertised (11)	{0, 1}	$(a_{i1t}, \ldots, a_{ipt}, \ldots, a_{iPt})$
	Page views of the blog	{1, 2, 3, ...}	Indegrees of the network
Followers	Favorite topics (29)	{0, 1}	$(u_{h1}, \ldots, u_{hk}, \ldots, u_{hK})$
	Favorite products (11)	{0, 1}	$(v_{h1}, \ldots, v_{hp}, \ldots, v_{hP})$
	Frequently visiting sites	{1, 2, 3, ...}	Outdegrees of the network

Note: The numbers in parentheses indicate the number of options for each corresponding item.

[4] It is important to note that the affiliate bloggers who responded to the first survey do not necessarily have a large number of actual followers, nor do the majority of them earn sufficient revenue from affiliate marketing, which suggests that many of them are not successful influencers.

Table 6.2 Optional values to weight the criteria used for network construction

Weights of Criteria	1	2	3	4	5	6	7
ω_1: Randomness	1	1/2	0	1/2	1/3	0	0
ω_2: Topic congruence	0	1/2	1	0	1/3	1/2	0
ω_3: Ad congruence	0	0	0	1/2	1/3	1/2	1

assigned to each follower agent. This extraction is repeated to generate 50 bootstrap samples.

2. Construction of Network: Given the seven possible combinations of $\boldsymbol{\omega} = (\omega_1, \omega_2, \omega_3)$, a link is created between the influencer and the follower generated in the first step.
3. Assignment of Advertising Mix Change Strategy: Based on the network created in the previous step, we compare all five levels of the random walker ratio (λ). Of influencers, $\lambda \times 100\%$ are randomly assigned to be the random walkers, and the remainder are assigned to be imitators. Once assigned, the strategy remains constant over time.
4. Iteration of Simulation: In accordance with the aforementioned simulation conditions, the agents engage in interactions with one another over a period of 30 time periods, wherein the decision-making process is repeated. To clarify, when their revenue decreases, influencers modify their advertising mix in accordance with the strategy they have been assigned. Followers visit one of the influencers they are following in each time period and choose the advertised product that matches their preferences for the product. This process is repeated 20 times.
5. Calculation of Affiliate Income: The number of purchases generated through affiliate marketing in each period of the simulation represents the revenue for that influencer.

6.2.5 When Affiliate Marketing Is more Successful

The size of the affiliate marketing market, which is the focus of this research, is evaluated based on the revenue generated by affiliate marketing facilitated by influencers. This may also be regarded as the welfare level enjoyed by their followers. In this model, the price of the product is fixed; thus, affiliate revenue is a function of the number of purchases made through affiliate marketing. As purchases are based on the autonomous preferences of followers, the more purchases there are, the more satisfied the followers are, unless there is uncertainty about the quality of the product. Figure 6.11 illustrates how the average affiliate revenue per influencer changes over time. It demonstrates the differences among the networks that connect influencers and followers and the differences in strategies for updating the ad mix.

First, we will examine the transition of revenue when the network is randomly formed, represented by $\boldsymbol{\omega} = (1,0,0)$ (Fig. 6.11a). From this, we can discern that although the affiliate revenue in the initial period is minimal, it shifts notably in the subsequent period, since the influencers alter their advertising mix if their revenues decrease from the preceding period. In the case where the majority of influencers are imitators ($\lambda = 0.1$), the average revenue increases monotonically and ultimately reaches a specific level. Conversely, if the majority are random walkers ($\lambda = 0.9$), the revenue experiences a brief period of sharp increase and subsequent fluctuations, ultimately reaching a higher level than in the case where the majority are imitators. Although not depicted in the figure, if λ exceeds 0.1, the pattern is nearly identical. Therefore, if a specific percentage or greater of random walkers are present, it can be inferred that the average affiliate revenue of the influencers will be higher.

Figure 6.11b illustrates the impact of $\boldsymbol{\omega} = (0, 1, 0)$ on revenue when influencers and followers are connected in a topic-congruent network. In the case where the majority of influencers are imitators ($\lambda = 0.1$), the pattern of revenue fluctuation is monotonically increasing, and this pattern does not seem to differ from that observed in 6.11a. Conversely, when the majority of influencers are random walkers ($\lambda = 0.9$), the fluctuation of average revenue is greater than that observed in 6.11a, and it gradually converges. The level at which it finally converges is slightly higher when there are a greater number of random walkers

The most prominent distinction can be observed when the network is ad-congruent (Fig. 6.11c: $\boldsymbol{\omega} = (0, 0, 1)$). In this scenario, the influencer offers an ad mix that matches most closely their followers' preferences, resulting in a notable initial affiliate revenue. However, when the influencer experiences a decline in revenue and searches for an alternative ad mix, their revenue exhibits greater fluctuations. In

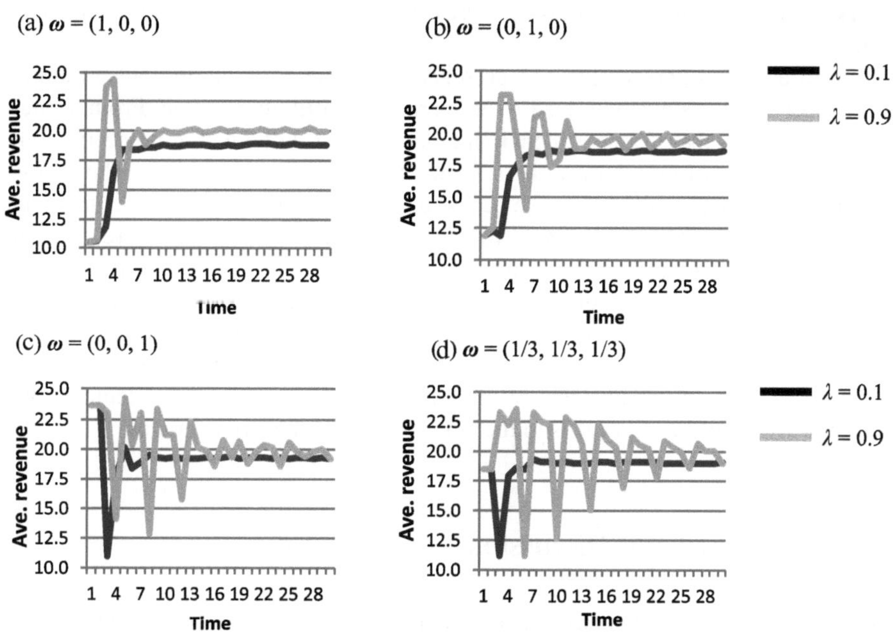

Fig. 6.11 Temporary changes in affiliate revenue per influencer

the case where the majority are imitators ($\lambda = 0.1$), convergence occurs rapidly, while in the case where the majority are random walkers ($\lambda = 0.9$), the fluctuations persist for an extended period before converging to a level that is lower than the initial level.

In the final analysis, we may consider the case where the network is constructed by equally considering the three criteria (Fig. 6.11d: $\boldsymbol{\omega} = (1/3, 1/3, 1/3)$). In the imitator-dominant case ($\lambda = 0.1$), the average revenue falls once and then immediately converges. Conversely, when random walkers are dominant ($\lambda = 0.9$), the fluctuations persist for a period, after which the imitators converge to a level commensurate with that observed when the majority of agents are imitators. It is hypothesized that as the proportion of random walkers increases, the time required for them to find the best solution also increases.

Fluctuations in affiliate revenue for influencers are to be expected in the initial period, but they will eventually stabilize once the advertising mix has been updated. It is therefore advisable to accumulate the revenue over a defined period of time in order to evaluate the overall impact on affiliate revenue. Figure 6.12 presents a comparison of the average cumulative revenue up to the 30th period for each simulation condition. The case where both randomness and ad-congruence are emphasized ($\boldsymbol{\omega} = (1/2, 0, 1/2)$) and where there are a high number of random walkers among influencers ($\lambda = 0.9$) has the highest cumulative revenue. Furthermore, in numerous networks, when the number of random walkers is exceedingly low ($\lambda = 0.1$), the cumulative revenue is markedly diminished. Consequently, it can be observed that the incorporation of randomness contributes to expanding the affiliate marketing market, both in influencer-follower networks and in strategies where influencers update their ad mix.

From a macro perspective, the presence of numerous random walkers among influencers will, on average, lead to an increase in affiliate revenue. From a micro perspective, it is therefore pertinent to inquire whether individual influencers should adopt the strategy of random walkers. Figure 6.13 illustrates the ratio of the average revenue of random walkers in each period divided by that of imitators (considering the cases of $\boldsymbol{\omega} = (0, 1, 0)$ and $\boldsymbol{\omega} = (0, 1/2, 1/2)$ with large cumulative revenue are taken up). It is evident that in the absence of a distinction between the two average revenues, the ratio will be equal to one. A review of the data in the figure reveals that the average revenue of the random walker exceeds that of the imitator in an early period. However, the difference between the two eventually diminishes. The imitator emulates the advertising mix of the random walker who initially demonstrated success, which ultimately leads to the convergence of the two averages.

6.3 Summary and Discussion

In Sect. 6.1, the mechanism by which influencers emerge from a population of originally symmetrical agents is modeled in the context of a competition to predict the success of a new product. When new products are introduced sequentially,

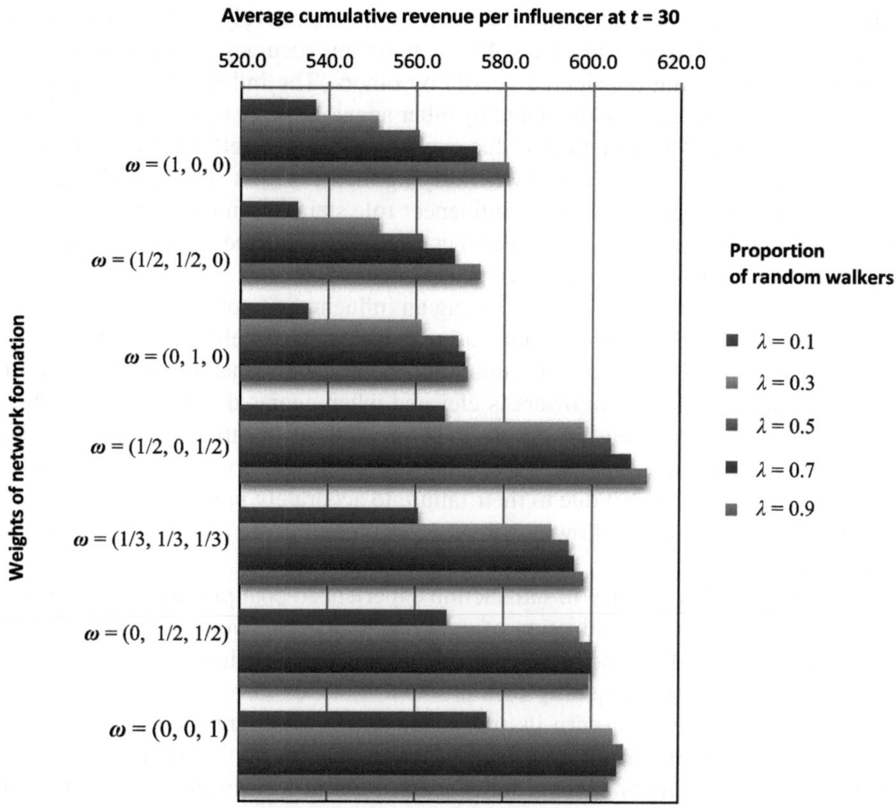

Fig. 6.12 Comparison of average cumulative revenue by types of influencer behavior

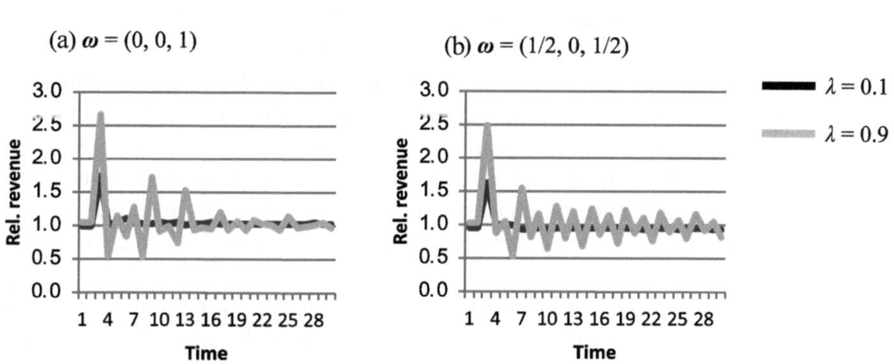

Fig. 6.13 Average revenue ratio per influencer for random walkers vs. imitators

consumers predict how successful they will be retrospectively, and if they predict success, they purchase the products. High prediction accuracy means being ahead of the trend and being considered "cool" by others. The influencers' influence is further amplified as they are emulated by other agents seeking to replicate their success in prediction. The initiation of this cycle results in the self-fulfilling nature of the influencer's predictions, thereby solidifying their position. The underlying reason for an agent's transition into an influencer role stems from their engagement in a competition for predictability, where they revise their degree of reliance on other agents and reconstruct their reference groups.

The phenomenon of an agent becoming an influencer is not entirely random. In this model, agents engage in communication regarding the likelihood of a new product's success. The results of the simulation demonstrate that the probability of increasing the number of followers is elevated when agents do not adhere to their own predictions and instead incorporate the predictions of others. Conversely, the probability of becoming an influencer is reduced when agents readily eliminate others from their reference list due to their failure to accurately predict outcomes. This suggests that a forgiving following strategy is optimal, given the random nature of prediction accuracy.

In reality, the discrepancy in satisfaction experienced post-purchase exerts a significant influence on the evaluation of the reliability of the word-of-mouth recommendations that led to the purchase. In circumstances where consumers face uncertainty regarding the quality of a product, it stands to reason that those who possess the capacity to discern its true quality will wield greater influence. This research makes a significant contribution by elucidating the mechanism through which certain consumers become influencers, even in the absence of factors that typically drive such influence, such as the ability to discern true quality (i.e., even in the context of convenience goods, where the true quality remains perpetually unknown).

Influencer marketing can be defined as a method of propagating word-of-mouth by seeding specific consumers who have become influencers (see Chap. 4 for more details). The unit cost of seeding influencers with a large number of followers is higher because, as a result of becoming more active and strategic, influencers attempt to monetize their influence. In addition to posting their own content on social media, a system called affiliate marketing has become increasingly prevalent, in which third-party advertisements are inserted, and the user is rewarded when they click on the advertisement or purchase the advertised product. In Sect. 6.2, a study using ABM that explored the mechanisms behind the growth of affiliate marketing was introduced.

Affiliate influencers choose the advertisements to be displayed on their websites, given the content they post. In doing so, they either adopt the strategy of imitating the advertising choices of influencers whose content is similar to their own or of those who earn the most, or they choose randomly. In addition to cases where consumers choose which influencers to follow based on their preferences for content, there are also cases where they are chosen at random or to maximize engagement with advertisements. As a result of the simulation, it was found that the overall reward increases if there is a certain percentage or more of influencers who chose advertisements at random ("random walker").

This indicates that even if influencers adopt an adaptive strategy based on their personal experiences, this alone will not necessarily lead to an increase in total affiliate revenue. Indeed, the revenue of individual influencers remains constant irrespective of the strategy they adopt concerning advertising. However, if a specific number of influencers randomly choose advertisements in a seemingly irrational manner, affiliate income as a whole experiences an increase. While this phenomenon may appear counterintuitive from a micro-level perspective, its macroscopic implications for market expansion and growth are noteworthy.

In the contemporary digital landscape, advertisements are progressively being delivered through the utilization of algorithms, prompting a shift in the adaptation strategies employed by affiliate influencers in structuring their content. The management of such alterations represents a subject that warrants further research. In this study, the preferences and behavioral constraints of influencers and followers are derived from web surveys. However, the absence of data concerning the network connections between influencers and followers necessitates further investigation. Additionally, the absence of macro-level data, such as click-through rates for affiliate advertising, limits the empirical output validation of the study. This research is classified as a medium-range model, occupying a position between the abstract model and the facsimile model, according to Gilbert's [59] classification.

The interaction between influencers and their followers can be conceptualized as a form of C2C (consumer-to-consumer) interaction. Perren and Kozinets [133] present the notion of "consociality" as a critical axis in the examination of C2C interaction.[5] They define consociality as "the physical and/or virtual copresence of social actors in a network, which provides an opportunity for social interaction between them." In this study, we adopt a broad perspective on C2C interaction, including contexts where direct economic exchange is not present, such as review platforms and social media. This framework is illustrated in Fig. 6.14, illuminating the dynamic relationship between influencers, defined as individuals with distinct personalities and characteristics, and consumers. Influencers serve as facilitators, inviting customers to engage in communication that ultimately leads to economic transactions. At the core of the provided diagram is the concept of the "influencer economy," wherein influencers assume a pivotal role. Influencers are individuals who possess distinct personalities and characteristics. They can establish a certain degree of consociality with consumers, thereby facilitating the transition from mere communication to economic exchange.

In order to demonstrate that this type of C2C interaction is facilitated by firms, it would be preferable to refer to it as a B2C2C economy. It appears inevitable that this will become a prominent feature of future business. In this case, the number of agents is substantial, and the types of agents cannot be handled by a simplistic

[5] Perren and Kozinets [133] also discuss "platform intermediation" as an additional axis in their classification, but the focus of this study will be on a different axis.

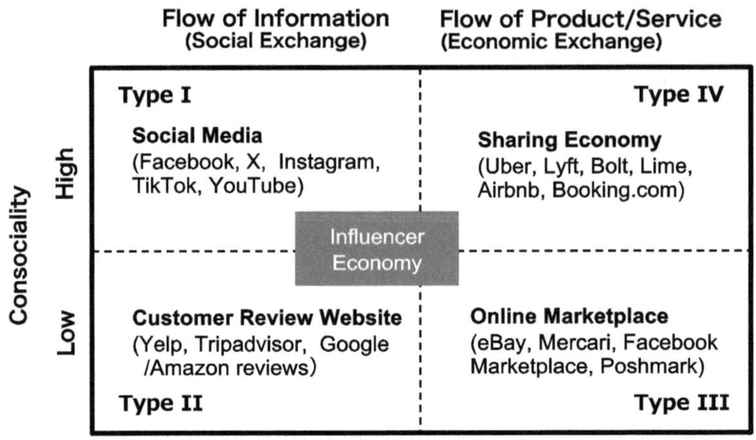

Fig. 6.14 Classification of C2C interactions. Note: This is a modified version of Fig. 6.1 in Mizuno et al. [113]

dichotomy of consumers and firms. Even if firms act to maximize profits, there are likely to be many agents with objective functions that are not necessarily limited to this. The process of their interaction with each other and pursuing their own objectives while receiving feedback from the macro-level state is exactly the kind of area that ABM is well-suited for. While ABM has been predominantly employed in the context of studying the diffusion of new products within marketing science, there is a growing anticipation for its application to a broader array of problems, including the B2C2C economy.

Afterword

In this book, we have examined agent-based modeling (ABM) research on consumer behavior from a marketing perspective. In the field of marketing science, ABM has predominantly been utilized to study the diffusion of new products. Throughout this book, we have compared the differences in the diffusion process—or the propagation of word-of-mouth—across various complex networks and analyzed its applications to influencer marketing, particularly seeding strategies. Additionally, we have introduced research cases that validate models using real data. Finally, we presented an example of ABM that assumes a scenario in which consumers not only share information with others but also proactively and strategically engage in communication.

At present, the application of ABM in marketing science is not necessarily active, and it is the purpose of this afterword to briefly discuss the issues that ABM currently faces in the marketing domain. The first issue is improving the level of empirical output validation as described by Rand and Rust [137]. In marketing, this means reproducing the macroscopic consumer behavior patterns. The advent of advanced analytical methods, such as machine learning, holds the potential to enhance the applicability of ABM in this domain by facilitating the integration of ABM with existing data resources. A notable approach that has been developed primarily for the financial market or macro economy data has demonstrated a substantial enhancement in its empirical validity (see [27, 28, 40, 103, 104, 135, 152, 164]) and may be introduced into the field of marketing.

However, the primary impediment to this transition is the absence of observations regarding the interaction between agents, an area where ABMs are most effective. The capacity to observe social interactions is constrained by online social media platforms, where data collection is often hindered by limited information on individual characteristics and purchasing behavior. One promising solution could involve a methodology similar to that proposed by Trusov et al. [162], which artificially generates a network between adopters in order to reproduce the observed diffusion process.

M. Mizuno, *Complex Modeling of Consumer Behavior*, Evolutionary Economics and Social Complexity Science 34,
https://doi.org/10.1007/978-4-431-54874-4

The second issue pertains to the enhancement of empirical input validation concerning the behavior of individual agents. One approach involves the incorporation of social interactions as variables in the estimation of individual behavioral models, employing marketing science or micro-econometrics, as explained in Sect. 5.2 of this book. However, this method may encounter limitations in capturing the dynamic interactions that ABMs are designed to capture. Another method involves conducting counterfactual simulations based on the results obtained from controlled experiments on test subjects. The combination of lab experiments and ABM is a methodology that is expected to evolve in the future (e.g., [153]). Furthermore, methods that utilize large-scale language models (LLMs) to enhance the realism of individual agent behaviors are beginning to be proposed, and they have the potential to bring about a fundamental shift in ABM methodologies [170].

The third issue pertains to the extension of ABM's application beyond the domains of product diffusion and word-of-mouth marketing. Previous studies have explored this extension; however, their development appears to be limited. The underlying reasons for this are multifaceted, but it is conceivable that the problem could be addressed without resorting to ABM or that alternative methods may be more efficacious. Nevertheless, there are also challenges that cannot be addressed through these means. For instance, ABM has been demonstrated to be highly effective in understanding the behavior of spatial competition models [79] between firms or between brands when the number of players is increased to more than two [126]. It is likely that there are other problems that can be solved without imposing unrealistic constraints using ABM, and it is hoped that ABM will be applied appropriately to such areas.

References

1. Anderson PW, Arrow KJ, Pines D, editors. *The economy as an evolving complex system.* Redwood City, CA: Addison-Wesley Publishing; 1988.
2. Aral S. *The hype machine: how social media disrupts our elections, our economy, and our health–and how we must adapt.* New York, NY: Penguin Random House; 2020.
3. Aral S, Dhillon PS. Social influence maximization under empirical influence models. *Nat Hum Behav.* 2018;2(6):375–82.
4. Aral S, Walker D. Identifying influential and susceptible members of social networks. *Science.* 2012;337(6092):337–41.
5. Arndt J. Product-related conversations in diffusion. *J Mark Res.* 1967;4(3):291–5.
6. Axelrod R. *The evolution of cooperation.* New York, NY: Basic Book; 1984.
7. Axelrod R. *The complexity of cooperation.* Princeton, NJ: Princeton University Press; 1997a.
8. Axelrod R. The dissemination of culture: a model with local convergence and global polarization. *J Confl Resolut.* 1997b;41:203–26.
9. Bakshy E, Hofman JM, Mason WA, Watts DJ. Everyone's an influencer: quantifying influence on twitter. In: *Proceedings of the fourth ACM international conference on web search and data mining*; 2011. p. 65–74.
10. Baños RA, Borge-Holthoefer J, Moreno Y. The role of hidden influentials in the diffusion of online information cascades. *EPJ Data Sci.* 2013;2(6):1–16.
11. Barabási A-L. *Linked: the new science of networks.* New York, NY: Perseus Books Group; 2002.
12. Barabási A-L, Albert R. Emergence of scaling in random networks. *Science.* 1999;286:509–12.
13. Bass FM. A new product growth for model consumer durables. *Manag Sci.* 1969;15(5):215–27.
14. Bauer F, Lizier JT. Identifying influential spreaders and efficiently estimating the number of infections in epidemic models: a path counting approach. *Europhys Lett.* 2012;99(6):68007.
15. Bearden WO, Netemeyer RG, Teel JE. Measurement of consumer susceptibility to interpersonal influence. J Consum Res. 1989;15(4):473–81.
16. Ben-Akiva M, Lerman SR. *Discrete choice analysis: theory and application to travel demand.* Boston, MA: MIT Press; 1985.
17. Berger J. Word of mouth and interpersonal communication: a review and directions for future research. J Consum Psychol. 2014;24(4):586–607.
18. Bhat CR. A Multiple Discrete-continuous extreme Value model: formulation and application to discretionary time-use decisions. Transport Res Part B. 2005;39(8):679–707.

M. Mizuno, *Complex Modeling of Consumer Behavior*, Evolutionary Economics and Social Complexity Science 34,
https://doi.org/10.1007/978-4-431-54874-4

19. Bhat CR. The Multiple Discrete-continuous Extreme Value (MDCEV) model: role of utility function parameters, identification considerations, and model extensions. Transport Res Part B. 2008;42(3):274–303.
20. Binmore K. The complexity of cooperation. *J Artif Soc Soc Simul.* 1998;1(1)
21. Bohlmann JD, Calantone RJ, Zhao M. The effects of market network heterogeneity on innovation diffusion: an agent-based modeling approach. *J Prod Innov Manag.* 2010;27(50):741–60.
22. Bowles S, Gintis H. *A cooperative species.* Princeton, NJ: Princeton University Press; 2011.
23. Brock WA, Durlauf SN. Interactions-based models. In: Heckman James J, Leamer Edward E, editors. *Handbook of econometrics*, 5, vol. 5. Amsterdam: North-Holland; 2001. p. 3297–380.
24. Broekhuizen TLJ, Delre SA. Torres A. Simulating the cinema market: how cross-cultural differences in social influence explain box office distributions. J Prod Innov Manag. 2011;28(2):204–17.
25. Broniec W, An S, Rugaber S, Goel AK. Guiding parameter estimation of agent-based modeling through knowledge-based function approximation. In: Proceedings of the AAAI 2021 Spring Symposium on Combining Machine Learning and Knowledge Engineering (AAAI-MAKE 2021); 2021.
26. Brown JJ, Reingen PH. Social ties and word-of-mouth referral behavior. J Consum Res. 1987;14(3):350–62.
27. Carrella E. No free lunch when estimating simulation parameters. J Artif Soc Soc Simul. 2021;24(2):1–7.
28. Carrella E, Bailey R, Madsen J. Calibrating agent-based models with linear regressions. J Artif Soc Soc Simul. 2020;23(1):7.
29. Casti JL. Would-be worlds: toward a theory of complex systems. Artif Life Robot. 1997;1:11–3.
30. Campbell C, Farrell JR. More than meets the eye: the functional components underlying influencer marketing. Bus Horiz. 2020;63(4):469–79.
31. Chan WKV, Hsu C. Service scaling on hyper-networks. Serv Sci. 2009;1(1):17–31.
32. Chan WKV, Gao B. Unfair consequence of fair competition in service systems—an agent-based and queueing approach. Serv Sci. 2013;5(3):249–62.
33. Chen W, Wang Y, Yang S. Efficient influence maximization in social networks. In: Proceedings of the 15th ACM SIGKDD international conference on knowledge discovery and data mining; 2009. p. 199–208.
34. Chen X, Van der Lans R, Phan TQ. Uncovering the importance of relationship characteristics in social networks: implications for seeding strategies. J Mark Res. 2017;54(2):187–201.
35. Chica M, Rand W. Building agent-based decision support systems for word-of-mouth programs: a freemium application. J Market Res. 2017;54(5):752–67.
36. Choi H, Kim S-H, Lee J. Role of network structure and network effects in diffusion of innovations. Ind Market Manag. 2010;39(1):170–7.
37. Coleman J, Katz E, Menzel H. The diffusion of an innovation among physicians. Sociometry. 1957;20(4):253–70.
38. D'Alessandro S, Johnson L, Gray D, Carter L. Consumer satisfaction versus churn in the case of upgrades of 3G to 4G cell networks. Mark Lett. 2015;26(4):489–500.
39. Deffuant G, Huet S. Propagation effects of filtering incongruent information. J Bus Res. 2007;60(8):816–25.
40. Dehkordi MA, Ebrahim JL, Ghorbani A, Nikolic I, Chappin E, Herder P. Using machine learning for agent specifications in agent-based models and simulations: a critical review and guidelines. J Artif Soc Soc Simul. 2023;26(1):9.
41. Delre SA, Broekhuizen TLJ, Bijmolt THA. The effects of shared consumption on product life cycles and advertising effectiveness: the case of the motion picture market. J Mark Res. 2016;53(April):608–27.
42. Delre SA, Jager W, Bijmolt THA, Janssen MA. Targeting and timing promotional activities: an agent-based model for the takeoff of new products. J Bus Res. 2007;60(8):826–35.

43. Delre SA, Jager W, Bijmolt THA, Janssen MA. Will it spread or not? The effects of social influences and network topology on innovation diffusion. J Prod Innov Manag. 2010;27(2):267–82.
44. Delre SA, Panico C, Wierenga B. Competitive strategies in the motion picture industry: an ABM to study investment decisions. Int J Res Mark. 2017;34(1):69–99.
45. Dost F, Sievert J, Kassima D. Revisiting firm-created word of mouth: high-value versus low-value seed selection. Int J Res Mark. 2016;33(1):236–9.
46. Dover Y, Goldenberg J, Shapira D. Network traces on penetration: uncovering degree distribution from adoption data. Mark Sci. 2012;31(4):689–712.
47. Dubois D, Bonezzi A, De Angelis M. Sharing with friends versus strangers: how interpersonal closeness influences word-of-mouth valence. J Mark Res. 2016;53(5):712–27.
48. Ebbes P, Huang Z, Rangaswamy A. Sampling designs for recovering local and global characteristics of social networks. Int J Res Mark. 2016;33(3):578–99.
49. Efron B, Tibshirani RJ. *An introduction to the bootstrap*. New York, NY: Chapman & Hall; 1993.
50. Eliashberg J, Shugan SM. Film critics: influencers or predictors? J Mark. 1997;61(April):68–78.
51. Erlandsson F, Bródka P, Borg A, Johnson H. Finding influential users in social media using association rule learning. Entropy. 2016;18(164):1–15.
52. Fabretti A. On the problem of calibrating an agent based model for financial markets. J Econ Interact Coord. 2013;8:277–93.
53. Farrell W. *How hits happen: forecasting predictability in a chaotic marketplace*. New York, NY: Harper Collins; 1998.
54. Garber T, Goldenberg J, Libai B, Muller E. From density to destiny: using spatial dimension of sales data for early prediction of new product success. Mark Sci. 2004;23(3):419–28.
55. Garcia R. Uses of agent-based modeling in innovation/new product development research. J Prod Innov Manag. 2005;22(5):380–98.
56. Garcia R, Rummel P, Hauser J. Validating agent-based marketing models through conjoint analysis. J Bus Res. 2007;60(8):848–57.
57. Gelper S, Van der Lans R, van Bruggen G. Competition for attention in online social networks: implications for seeding strategies. Manag Sci. 2021;67(2):1026–47.
58. Gerrath MHEE, Usrey B. The impact of influencer motives and commonness perceptions on follower reactions toward incentivized reviews. Int J Mark Res. 2021;38(3):531–48.
59. Gilbert N. *Agent-based models*. Thousand Oaks, CA: Sage Publications; 2008.
60. Gladwell M. The tipping point: how little things can make a big difference. New York, NY: Little Brown; 2006.
61. Godes D, Mayzlin D. Firm-created word-of-mouth communication: evidence from a field test. Mark Sci. 2009;28(4):721–39.
62. Goldenberg J, Han S, Lehmann DR, Hong JW. The role of hubs in the adoption process. J Mark. 2009;73(2):1–13.
63. Goldenberg J, Libai B, Moldovan S, Muller E. The NPV of bad news. Int J Res Mark. 2007;24(3):186–200.
64. Goldenberg J, Libai B, Muller E. Talk of the network: a complex systems look at the underlying process of word-of-mouth. Mark Lett. 2001;12(3):211–23.
65. Goldenberg J, Libai B, Muller E. Riding the saddle: how cross-market communications can create a major slump in sales. J Mark. 2002;66(2):1–16.
66. Goldenberg J, Libai B, Muller E. The chilling effects of network externalities. Int J Res Mark. 2010;27(1):4–15.
67. Goldenberg J, Libai B, Solomon S, Jan N, Stauffer D. Marketing percolation. Phys A: Stat Mech Appl. 2000;284(1–4):335–47.
68. Goldenberg J, Lowengart O, Shapira D. Zooming in: self-emergence of movements in new product growth. Mark Sci. 2009;28(2):274–92.

69. Gong S, Zhang J, Zhao P, Jiang X. Tweeting as a marketing tool: a field experiment in the TV industry. J Mark Res. 2017;54(6):833–50.
70. Granovetter MS. The strength of weak ties. Am J Sociol. 1973;78(6):1360–80.
71. Granovetter M. Threshold models of collective behavior. Am J Sociol. 1978;83(6):1420–43.
72. Guadagni PM, Little JDC. A logit model of brand choice calibrated on scanner data. Mark Sci. 1983;2(3):203–38.
73. Haenlein M, Anadol E, Farnsworth T, Hugo H, Hunichen J, Welte D. Navigating the new era of influencer marketing: how to be successful on Instagram, TikTok, and Co. Calif Manag Rev. 2020;63(1):5–25.
74. Haenlein M, Libai B. Targeting revenue leaders for a new product. J Mark. 2013;77(3):65–80.
75. Heider F. Attitudes and cognitive organization. J Psychol. 1946;21:107–12.
76. Hill RP, Watkins A. The profit implications of altruistic versus egoistic orientations for business-to-business exchanges. Int J Res Mark. 2009;26(1):52–9.
77. Hinz O, Skiera B, Barrot C, Becker JU. Seeding strategies for viral marketing: an empirical comparison. J Mark. 2011;75(6):55–71.
78. Hoffman DL, Novak TP. How to acquire customers on the web. Harv Bus Rev. 2000;78(3):179–83.
79. Hotelling H. Stability in competition. Econ J. 1929;39(153):41–57.
80. Hu Y, Ji S, Jin Y, Ling Feng H, Stanley E, Havlin S. Local structure can identify and quantify influential global spreaders in large scale social networks. Proc Natl Acad Sci. 2018a;115(29):7468–72.
81. Hu H-H, Lin J, Qian Y, Sun J. Strategies for new product diffusion: whom and how to target? J Bus Res. 2018b;83:111–9.
82. Hughes C, Swaminathan V, Brooks G. Driving brand engagement through online social influencers: an empirical investigation of sponsored blogging campaigns. J Mark. 2019;83(5):78–96.
83. Izquierdo SS, Izquierdo LR. The impact of quality uncertainty without asymmetric information on market efficiency. J Bus Res. 2007;60(8):858–67.
84. Iyengar R, Han S, Gupta S. Do friends influence purchases in a social network?. *Harvard Business School Discussion Paper*, (Feb 26); 2009. p. 1–34.
85. Iyengar R, Van den Bulte C, Valente TW. Opinion leadership and social contagion in new product diffusion. Mark Sci. 2011;30(2):195–212.
86. Katz E, Lazarsfeld PF. *Personal influence: the part played by people in the flow of mass communications*. Glencoe, IL: Free Press; 1955.
87. Katz ML, Shapiro C. Network externalities, competition, and compatibility. Am Econ Rev. 1985;75(3):424–40.
88. Kempe D, Kleinberg J, Tardos É. Maximizing the spread of influence through a social network. In: *Proceedings of the ninth ACM SIGKDD international conference on knowledge discovery and data mining*; 2003. p. 137–46.
89. Kim DA, Hwong AR, Derek Stafford D, Alex Hughes A, O'Malley J, Fowler JH, Christakis NA. Social network targeting to maximise population behaviour change: a cluster randomised controlled trial. Lancet. 2015;386(9989):145–53.
90. King CW, Summers JO. Overlap of opinion leadership across consumer product categories. J Mark Res. 1971;7(1):43–50.
91. Kranzbühler A-M, Zerres A, Kleijnen MHP, Verlegh PWJ. Beyond valence: a meta-analysis of discrete emotions in firm-customer encounters. J Acad Mark Sci. 2020;48(3):478–98.
92. Kübler RV, Colicev A, Pauwels KH. Social media's impact on the consumer mindset: when to use which sentiment extraction tool? J Interact Mark. 2020;50:136–55.
93. Kumar V, Bhaskaran V, Mirchandani R, Shah M. Practice prize winner—creating a measurable social media marketing strategy: increasing the value and ROI of intangibles and tangibles for Hokey Pokey. Mark Sci. 2013;32(2):194–212.
94. Kwak H, Lee C, Park H, Moon S. What is Twitter, a social network or a news media? In: *Proceedings of the 19th international conference on World Wide Web*; 2010. p. 591–600.

95. Lambrecht A, Tucker C, Wiertz C. Advertising to early trend propagators: evidence from Twitter. Mark Sci. 2017;37(2):177–99.
96. Lanz A, Goldenberg J, Shapira D, Stahl F. Climb or jump: status-based seeding in user-generated content networks. J Mark Res. 2019;56(3):361–78.
97. Leibenstein H. Bandwagon, Snob, and Veblen effects in the theory of consumers' demand. Q J Econ. 1950;64(2):183–207.
98. Leskovec J, Krause A, Guestrin C, Faloutsos C, VanBriesen J, Glance N. Cost-effective outbreak detection in networks. In: *Proceedings of the 13th ACM SIGKDD international conference on knowledge discovery and data mining*; 2007. p. 420–9.
99. Leung FF, Gu FF, Palmatier RW. Online influencer marketing. J Acad Mark Sci. 2022;50:1–26.
100. Libai B, Muller E, Peres R. The role of seeding in multi-market entry. Int J Res Mark. 2005;22(4):375–93.
101. Libai B, Biyalogorsky E, Gerstner E. Setting referral fees in affiliate marketing. J Serv Res. 2003;5(4):303–15.
102. Libai B, Muller E, Peres R. Decomposing the value of word-of-mouth seeding programs: acceleration versus expansion. J Mark Res. 2013;50(2):161–76.
103. Lux T. Estimation of agent-based models using sequential Monte Carlo methods. J Econ Dyn Control. 2018;91:391–408.
104. Lux T. Bayesian estimation of agent-based models via adaptive particle Markov Chain Monte Carlo. Comput Econ. 2021;60:451–77.
105. McFadden D. Conditional logit analysis of qualitative choice behavior. In: Zarembka P, editor. *Frontiers in econometrics*. New York, NY: Academic Press; 1974.
106. McFadden D. Economic choices. Am Econ Rev. 2001;91(3):351–78.
107. Menczer F, Fortunato S, Davis CA. *A first course in network science*. Cambridge: Cambridge University Press; 2020.
108. Michalski R, Kajdanowicz T, Bródka P, Kazienko P. Seed selection for spread of influence in social networks: temporal vs. static approach. New Gener Comput. 2014;32(3):213–35.
109. Min B, Liljeros F, Makse HA. Finding influential spreaders from human activity beyond network location. PLOS ONE. 2015;10(8):1–13.
110. Midgley D, Marks R, Kunchamwar D. Building and assurance of agent-based models: an example and challenge to the field. J Bus Res. 2007;60(8):884–93.
111. Mizuno M. How consumer-generated advertising works: an empirical agent-based simulation. In: Chen S-H, Terano T, Yamamoto R, Tai C-C, editors. *Advances in computational social science, the 4th World Congress (Agent-Based Social Systems)*. Springer; 2014. p. 17–30.
112. Mizuno M, Abe M, Shinbo N. Seeding strategies in influencer marketing accounting for the heterogeneity of receivers and senders. J Mark Sci. 2022;30(1):9–32. [in Japanese]
113. Mizuno M, Onishi H, Shibuya S, Yamamoto H. C2C interactions under the digital media environment–a review and perspective. J Mark Sci. 2018;26(1):7–39. [in Japanese]
114. Mizuno M, Inoue S, Noguchi M. Emergence of the leader-follower structure among consumers: what type of consumers would be the most influential in the marketplace? In: Takahashi S, Sallach D, Rouchier J, editors. *Advancing social simulation: the First World Congress (Post-Proceedings of The First World Congress on Social Simulation (WCSS06))*. Springer; 2007. p. 117–28.
115. Mizuno M, Mori T, Baba T, Takakai Y, Sera K. Dynamics of new product diffusion and word-of-mouth: an agent-based modeling based on empirical data. J Mark Sci. 2011;19(1):91–109. [in Japanese]
116. Mizuno M, Nishiyama N. Interacting TV viewers: a case of empirical agent-based modeling and simulation for business applications. Adv Complex Syst. 2003;6(3):361–73.
117. Moore GA. *Crossing the chasm: marketing and selling high-tech products to mainstream customers*. New York, NY: Harper Business; 1991.
118. Mukherjee P. How chilling are network externalities? The role of network structure. Int J Res Mark. 2014;31(4):452–6.

119. Muller E. Innovation diffusion, in Chapter 4. In: Winer RS, Neslin SA, editors. *The history of marketing science*. Singapore: World Scientific; 2014.
120. Muller E, Peres R. The effect of social networks structure on innovation performance: a review and directions for research. Int J Res Mark. 2019;36(1):3–19.
121. Nejad MG, Amini M, Babakus E. Success factors in product seeding: the role of homophily. J Retail. 2015;91(1):68–88.
122. Nejad MG, Amini M, Sherrell DL. The profit impact of revenue heterogeneity and assortativity in the presence of negative word-of-mouth. Int J Res Mark. 2016;33(3):656–73.
123. Nelson RR, Winter SG. *An evolutionary theory of economic change*. Cambridge, MA: The Belknap Press of Harvard University Press; 1982.
124. Newman M. *Networks*. 2nd ed. New York, NY: Oxford University Press; 2018.
125. Nowak MA. *Evolutionary dynamics: exploring the equations of life*. Cambridge, MA: Harvard University Press; 2006.
126. Ottino-Loffler B, Stonedahl F, Veetil V, Wilensky U. Spatial competition with interacting agents. Int J Microsimulation. 2017;10(3):75–91.
127. Papatla P, Bhatnagar A. Choosing the right mix of on-line affiliates: how do you select the best? J Advert. 2002;16(3):69–81.
128. Payne JW, Bettman JR, Johnson EJ. *The adaptive decision maker: effort and accuracy in choice*. Cambridge: Cambridge University Press; 1997.
129. Pei A, Mayzlin D. Influencing social media influencers through affiliation. Mark Sci. 2021;41(3):593–615.
130. Pei S, Muchnik L, Andrade JS, Zheng Z, Makse HA. Searching for superspreaders of information in real-world social media. Sci Rep. 2014;4(1):5547.
131. Peres R, Muller E, Mahajan V. Innovation diffusion and new product growth models: a critical review and research directions. Int J Res Mark. 2010;27(2):91–106.
132. Peres R, Van den Bulte C. When to take or forgo new product exclusivity: balancing protection from competition against word-of-mouth spillover. J Mark. 2014;78(2):83–100.
133. Perren R, Kozinets RV. Lateral exchange markets: how social platforms operate in a networked economy. J Mark. 2018;82(1):20–36.
134. Phan TQ, Godes D. The evolution of influence through endogenous link formation. Mark Sci. 2018;37(2):259–78.
135. Platt D. A comparison of economic agent-based model calibration methods. J Econ Dyn Control. 2020;113:103859.
136. Rahmandad H, Sterman J. Heterogeneity and network structure in the dynamics of diffusion: comparing agent-based and differential equation models. Manag Sci. 2008;54(5):998–1014.
137. Rand W, Rust RT. Agent-based modeling in marketing: guidelines for rigor. Int J Res Mark. 2011;28(3):181–93.
138. Rand W, Stummer C. Agent-based modeling of new product market diffusion: an overview of strengths and criticisms. Ann Oper Res. 2021;305(1):425–47.
139. Rapoport A, Seale DA, Colman AM. Is tit-for-tat the answer? On the conclusions drawn from Axelrod's tournaments. PLOS ONE. 2015;10(7):e0134128.
140. Reingen PH, Foster BL, Brown JJ, Seidman SB. Brand congruence in interpersonal relations: a social network analysis. J Consum Res. 1984;11(3):771–83.
141. Rogers EM. *Diffusion of innovations (1st/5th edition)*. New York: Free Press; 1962/2003.
142. Rogers EM, Cartano DG. Methods of measuring opinion leadership. Public Opin Q. 1962;26(3):435–41.
143. Rosen E. *The anatomy of buzz: how to create word of mouth marketing*. New York, NY: Doubleday; 2002.
144. Rossman G, Fisher JC. Network hubs cease to be influential in the presence of low levels of advertising. Proc Natl Acad Sci. 2021;118(7):1–4.
145. Rust RT, Kamakura W, Alpert MI. Viewer preference segmentation and viewing choice models for network television. J Advert. 1992;21(1):1–18.

146. Salganik MJ, Dodds PS, Watts DJ. Experimental study of inequality and unpredictability in an artificial cultural market. Science. 2006;311(5762):854–6.
147. Sayama H. Introduction to the modeling and analysis of complex systems, Geneseo, NY: Open SUNY Textbook; 2015.
148. Schelling TC. Dynamic models of segregation. J Math Sociol. 1971;1(2):143–86.
149. Schelling TC. *Micromotives and macrobehavior*. New York, NY: WW Norton and Company; 1978.
150. Schenk TA, Löffler G, Rauh J. Agent-based simulation of consumer behavior in grocery shopping on a regional level. J Bus Res. 2007;60(8):894–903.
151. Schutte S. Optimization and falsification in empirical agent-based models. J Artif Soc Soc Simul. 2010;13(1):2.
152. Shiono T. Estimation of agent-based models using Bayesian deep learning approach of BayesFlow. J Econ Dyn Control. 2021;125:104082.
153. Smith EB, Rand W. Simulating macro-level effects from micro-level observations. Manag Sci. 2018;64(11):5405–21.
154. Stephen AT, Lehmann DR. How word-of-mouth transmission encouragement affects consumers' transmission decisions, receiver selection, and diffusion speed. Int J Res Mark. 2016;33(4):755–66.
155. Sun J, Feng L, Mingwei D, Ma X, Fan Z, Gloor P, Yanqing H. Ultra-efficient information detection on large-scale online social networks. Phys. A: Stat Mech Appl. 2021;581:126204.
156. Tay NSP, Lusch RF. A preliminary test of Hunt's general theory of competition: using artificial adaptive agents to study complex and ill-defined environments. J Bus Res. 2005;58(9):1155–68.
157. Tesfatsion L, Judd KL. *Handbook of computational economics: agent-based computational economics*. Amsterdam, NL: North-Holland; 2006.
158. Törnberg P. How digital media drive affective polarization through partisan sorting. Proc Natl Acad Sci. 2022;119(42):e2207159119.
159. Toubia O, Goldenberg J, Garcia R. Improving penetration forecasts using social interactions data. Manag Sci. 2014;60(12):3049–66.
160. Toubia O, Stephen AT, Freud A. Viral marketing: a large-scale field experiment. Econ Manag Financ Mark. 2011;66(3):43–65.
161. Trusov M, Bodapati AV, Bucklin RE. Determining influential users in internet social networks. J Mark Res. 2010;47(4):643–58.
162. Trusov M, Rand W, Joshi YV. Improving prelaunch diffusion forecasts: using synthetic networks as simulated priors. J Mark Res. 2013;50(6):675–90.
163. Vag A. Simulating changing consumer preferences: a dynamic conjoint model. J Bus Res. 2007;60(8):904–11.
164. van der Hoog S. Surrogate modelling in (and of) agent-based models: a prospectus. Comput Econ. 2019;53(3):1245–63.
165. van Eck PS, Jager W, Leeflang PSH. Opinion leaders' role in innovation diffusion: a simulation study. J Prod Innov Manag. 2011;28(2):187–203.
166. Watts DJ, Dodds PS. Influentials, networks, and public opinion formation. J Consum Res. 2007;34(4):441–58.
167. Watts DJ, Strogatz SH. Collective dynamics of "Small-World" networks. Nature. 1998;393(4):440–2.
168. Weng J, Lim E-P, Jiang J. TwitterRank: finding topic-sensitive influential Twitters. In: *Proceedings of the third ACM international conference on Web Search and Data Mining*; 2010. p. 261–70.
169. Winer RS, Neslin SA, editors. The history of marketing science. Singapore: World Scientific; 2014.
170. Wu Z, Peng R, Xu H, Zheng S, Zhang Y, Xiao C. Smart agent-based modeling: on the use of large language models in computer simulations. *arXiv preprint arXiv:2311.06330*; 2023.
171. Zhang T, Nuttall WJ. Evaluating government's policies on promoting smart metering diffusion in retail electricity markets via agent-based simulation. J Prod Innov Manag. 2011;28(2):169–86.

172. Zhang T, Gensler S, Garcia R. A study of the diffusion of alternative fuel vehicles: an agent-based modeling approach. J Prod Innov Manag. 2011;28(2):152–68.
173. Zhang T, Zhang D. Agent-based simulation of consumer purchase decision-making and the decoy effect. J Bus Res. 2007;60(8):912–22.
174. Zhang T, Dong P, Zeng Y, Yanbing J. Analyzing the diffusion of competitive smart wearable devices: an agent-based multi-dimensional relative agreement model. J Bus Res. 2022;139:90–105.

MIX
Papier aus verantwortungsvollen Quellen
Paper from responsible sources
FSC® C105338

If you have any concerns about our products,
you can contact us on
ProductSafety@springernature.com

In case Publisher is established outside the EU,
the EU authorized representative is:
Springer Nature Customer Service Center GmbH
Europaplatz 3, 69115 Heidelberg, Germany

Printed by Libri Plureos GmbH
in Hamburg, Germany